Global Outlook
High Intermediate Reading

Brenda Bushell and Brenda Dyer

D1226080

McGraw Hill

Boston   Burr Ridge, IL   Dubuque, IA   Madison, WI   New York   San Francisco   St. Louis
Bangkok   Bogotá   Caracas   Kuala Lumpur   Lisbon   London   Madrid   Mexico City
Milan   Montreal   New Delhi   Santiago   Seoul   Singapore   Sydney   Taipei   Toronto

The **McGraw·Hill** Companies

Global Outlook 1

Published by McGraw-Hill/Contemporary, a business unit of The McGraw-Hill
Companies, Inc., 1221 Avenue of the Americas, New York, NY 10020. Copyright © 2003
by The McGraw-Hill Companies, Inc. All rights reserved. No part of this publication
may be reproduced or distributed in any form or by any means, or stored in a database
or retrieval system, without the prior written consent of The McGraw-Hill Companies,
Inc., including, but not limited to, in any network or other electronic storage or
transmission, or broadcast for distance learning.
Some ancillaries, including electronic and print components, may not be available to
customers outside the United States.

10 09 08 07 06 05 04 03
20 09 08 07 06 05 04
CTF   ANL

Cover image: © *Leon Zernitsky*

When ordering this title, use ISBN 007- 255312-X

Printed in Singapore

TABLE OF CONTENTS

INTRODUCTION

Global Outlook 1 is designed to introduce high-intermediate learners of English as a Foreign or Second Language to the basic reading skills required for fluent, accurate reading in English.

Global Outlook 1 is the first book in a two-level series. The key features of the Global Outlook series are high-interest content, careful sequencing of reading skills, and oral communication extension activities which encourage students to go beyond the reading text and consider how the issues impact their lives.

Students will:

- Acquire reading skills which fluent readers of English use unconsciously

- Learn to use their background knowledge to understand a text

- Develop the ability to read chunks of information for general understanding instead of reading and translating word-for-word

- Expand their knowledge and build a global perspective of world issues and social trends.

Global Outlook is designed for both teachers who are experienced in teaching reading skills but looking for new ways to implement them, and those who are less experienced and are looking for guidance on how to incorporate specific reading-skill development in their language classes.

▶APPROACHES TO TEACHING READING

One of the keys to teaching reading effectively is to present high-interest, provocative reading material which will engage the reader. The readings have been carefully chosen to include a variety of viewpoints on global topics centered around social issues, the environment, psychology, business, and technology. The readings also include various styles: journalism (newspaper and magazines), interviews, advertisements, fiction, poetry, and academic essays. The readings, though diverse, share the common theme of global content. Vocabulary and concepts related to global education are recycled throughout the text, building up a basic core of knowledge. When topics are integrated rather than randomly presented, general comprehension is facilitated.

Reading skills are carefully presented and practiced. One of the common stumbling blocks for second and foreign-language students is their use of "bottom-up" information processing, that is, word-by-word translation of the text for comprehension. This is not efficient and often leads to slow, inaccurate reading. *Global Outlook* emphasizes the top-down reading process, in which the reader uses what he or she already knows in trying to comprehend the text. Pre-reading exercises, finding the main idea, and vocabulary in context exercises are examples of how this textbook reinforces efficient top-down reading strategies.

The skills of the reading process are articulated for the student in each unit. Research shows that it is possible to divide reading into a series of sub-processes and students can be trained in specific reading comprehension skills which they can transfer to new reading situations. Students learn about the reading process itself, and begin to realize that "reading" is not the same thing as "translating." Skill-focus highlights the thinking processes which good English readers use in understanding a text in English. This meta-cognitive awareness is an important basis for language acquisition in adult learners. Therefore, the *process* of comprehending should be the purpose of each unit.

➤ UNIT ORGANIZATION

The following exercises are included in each unit. The sequence of exercises may vary from unit to unit, depending on the reading skill which is targeted.

Before You Begin: In this section, students are asked to think about the topic of the reading and make predictions. By previewing, students recall information to begin the cognitive process of matching new information with what is already known. This enhances reading comprehension not only by sparking interest, but by building content and vocabulary schema.

Getting the Main Idea: This is an important top-down reading skill that requires students to actively process global information as they read, without getting distracted by details. Students learn to use the pre-reading information they have gathered from the Before You Begin section to access the main point of the reading while reading for the first time. Rhetorical strategies for locating the main idea are especially targeted in Unit 5, but practice for this very important skill is given in each unit.

Vocabulary in Context: One of the most important reading skills of this text is the ability to guess the meaning of unknown words from context. Students often depend on their dictionaries too much, which slows down their reading speed and interferes with comprehension. Using cues such as grammatical and semantic context, punctuation, and transitions, students can become confident in inferring the meaning of key words.   In order for this exercise to be effective, students must NOT use their dictionaries.

Reading Skill: One particular reading skill is targeted in each unit. Each reading is accompanied by a specific reading skill description and exercise. These reading skills are unconscious in fluent English readers, but they can be learned. By becoming aware of these reading processes, students will become more effective readers.

Taking a Closer Look: The ability to find important information is developed through the practice of scanning. Students learn how to search quickly to extract certain specific information without reading through the whole text. For academic English, scanning is absolutely essential. In vocational or daily English, scanning is useful in dealing with schedules, manuals, forms, and other list-oriented reading genres.

Communicate: One of the unique features of this reading text is that the reading is supported by speaking. Each unit is followed by a "Communicate" speaking activity. In the speaking activity, students are given a chance to personalize the text, that is, make connections between the readings and their own lives and opinions. It is a good opportunity to recycle unit vocabulary. For teachers concerned with values education, this section gives students a chance to develop their opinions of the ideas presented in the readings and also raises their awareness of the diversity of values and beliefs of their classmates. Finally, when students realize that this is a post-reading component of each unit, they tend to approach the readings more critically, forming judgments and opinions of the content they will share with their classmates. In other words, it becomes a built-in motivator for reading.

Interactive Journal Response: These final questions provide another chance for vocabulary recycling, and closure for each unit. Students are asked to interpret the information of the reading, give their opinions, and respond. We have chosen provocative topics which we hope students will respond to by agreeing or disagreeing. One of the purposes of the text is to empower students to become independent, critical thinkers and readers. The instruction is for students to choose one question and write a response. This could be collected by teachers as a check of reading comprehension. Other options are for students to paraphrase their response orally with a partner, or in small groups in the following class as a warm-up activity. The exercise is not intended to be a formal writing exercise, but rather a final communicative activity to support the students' reading comprehension. If students feel that their reactions to and opinions of the readings are valued, their motivation for reading future units will be enhanced.

THE GLOBAL VILLAGE

This textbook focuses on current views on topics from around the world. You will be developing your English skills by reading, speaking, and writing about each topic. You will also have the opportunity to explore your own views about these topics.

The reading of Unit 1 presents the idea of a "global village" where cultures and customs flow across borders.

READING

➤ BEFORE YOU BEGIN

1. The following key words appear in the reading. Look them up in the dictionary to complete the chart below:

	Part of speech	Definition
globe		
global		
globalization		

2. What do you think "global village" means?

3. Are you part of the global village? Check (✓) the appropriate boxes. The teacher will record the results on the board.

How often do you . . .

	Never	Sometimes	Often
1. eat food from other countries?			
2. buy clothing made outside your country?			
3. buy CDs by musicians from other countries?			
4. watch movies from other countries?			
5. talk with people of other cultures?			

4. Some words have become commonly used around the world. Do you know which languages the following words came from originally? Match the words with their origins.

Word	Language of origin
karaoke	French
yoga	English (with Greek root origin)
pizza	Japanese
taxi	French
hotel	Sanskrit
disco	Italian

(A line connects "karaoke" to "Japanese.")

➤ AS YOU READ

Read "The Global Village Finally Arrives" through quickly one time to get an idea of what the reading is about.

THE GLOBAL VILLAGE FINALLY ARRIVES
by Pico Iyer (from *Time International*)

1   This is a typical day of a typical person in today's world. I wake up to the sound of my Japanese clock radio and put on a T-shirt sent to me by an uncle in Nigeria. On TV, the morning news is in Mandarin; on the radio, the results of the baseball game are in Korean. I walk out into the street, past German cars, to my office. 5 The street has a Spanish name. Around me are English-language students from Korea, Switzerland, and Argentina. For lunch I can walk to a sushi bar, a tandoori[1] restaurant, a Thai café, or a burrito joint[2] (run by an old Japanese lady). Who am I?, I sometimes wonder. And where am I? 10

2   I am the son of Indian parents. I am a British citizen who spends much of his time in Japan. And now I am in Southern California, in a quiet city, but I could as easily be in Vancouver or Sydney or London or Hong Kong. The whole planet, you might say, is going global. More and more of the globe looks like America, but America 15 itself is looking more and more like the rest of the globe. A common

---
[1] *tandoori:* food cooked in a special Indian oven called a tandoor
[2] *burrito joint:* a small, inexpensive restaurant that serves Mexican food

multiculturalism[3] links us all. "Taxi" and "hotel" and "disco" are universal terms now, but so are "karaoke" and "yoga" and "pizza." For the gourmet, there is tiramisu at the Burger King in Kyoto, pasta in Saigon, and enchiladas on every menu in Nepal.   20

3   News, clothing, food, and even languages are moving across borders in the diversified world of the twenty-first century. But not only these things are mingling. In Brussels, one new baby in every four is Arab. In Japan, one can rub shoulders with[4] Iranians, British, Pakistanis, and Filipinos. When people move around the globe, cultural values go   25 with them. New immigrants[5] from Taiwan, Vietnam, and India import values of hard work and family closeness to America, while at the same time America sends its values[6] of upward mobility[7] and individualism to Taipei and Ho Chi Minh City and Mumbai.

4   None of this, of course, is new. Since ancient times, humans have   30 made journeys to faraway towns and countries, and exchanged goods and ideas. But now, all these cultures are crossing at the speed of light and making their way to sleepy villages on all the continents of the world. Although it is exciting, there are dangers in this globalization. Some traditions and customs are being changed, or even lost. While   35 some places in the world are wired for international communication, others remain isolated. The world may become even more divided, into the "haves" and the "have nots." Today as I eat my sushi in California, I wonder about my future in this global village.

---

[3] *multiculturalism:* mixed cultures

[4] *rubbing shoulders with:* associating with

[5] *immigrants:* people from another country coming to live in a new country

[6] *values:* principles or beliefs held to be important by an individual or society

[7] *upward mobility:* the idea that one can move into a higher level of society by making more money

➤ **READING SKILL: Skimming**

Skimming is reading quickly to get the main idea. Good readers often skim an article first, before reading it again more slowly and carefully. An effective skimming rate is 800 words per minute. Here are some tips for skimming:

- Let your eyes move quickly over the paragraphs. Do not read every word and sentence.

- Read the first and last paragraph.

- Read the first and last sentence of each paragraph.

- Do not use your dictionary!

➤ READING SKILL PRACTICE: Skimming

Take 35 seconds to skim Reading One.

1. Skim each paragraph, letting your eyes move over the words quickly. Notice the first and last sentences of each paragraph.

2. Then underline the first and last sentences of each paragraph. Notice how they give the general idea of the passage.

➤ GETTING THE MAIN IDEA

Skim the paragraphs indicated in brackets. Then decide if the following statements are true (**T**) or false (**F**). Compare your answers with your classmates.

1. _____ The author is an unusual person, living in a strange city. [1]

2. _____ Today, food and language cross borders, making a global culture. [2]

3. _____ The global culture is American. [2]

4. _____ Values of different cultures are flowing across borders. [3]

5. _____ American values are taking over the world. [3]

6. _____ Globalization may have some bad effects. [4]

➤ VOCABULARY IN CONTEXT

The following sentences contain vocabulary from the reading. Read each sentence and circle the best synonym or definition for the highlighted word. Look at the reading for clues to help you guess the meaning. Do not use your dictionary.

1. There was **universal** agreement that we would all go to the movies instead of finishing our homework. [Check back to paragraph 2 for another example of how *universal* is used]

   a. individual

   b. common

   c. some

2. He was chosen as the **gourmet** of our group because he always prepared delicious food when we came to visit. [paragraph 2]

    a. person who is an expert on food

    b. person who eats too much

    c. person who wants to throw away food

3. The assignments were **diversified** so the students would not become bored. [paragraph 3]

    a. made exactly the same

    b. given a variety of difference

    c. hidden or kept secret

4. People at the party were **mingling** in order to get to know one another. [paragraph 3]

    a. mixing

    b. separating

    c. ignoring

5. The company wanted to **import** clothing from India into the US because it is cheaper. [paragraph 3]

    a. use up

    b. bring in

    c. take out

6. They felt **isolated** from society because they did not own a radio or TV. [paragraph 4]

    a. joined

    b. separated

    c. mixed

➤ TAKING A CLOSER LOOK

Part A

The reading gives examples of how the world has become a global village.

1. Find examples from the reading that support this point.

2. Write those examples in the appropriate columns in the chart below. One is done for you.

3. Check your examples with your partner.

Food	Language	Values	Products
			German car

Part B

Read "The Global Village Finally Arrives" again, this time focusing on details. Circle the best answer, then underline the phrase or sentence in the reading that supports your answer. Compare your answers with your classmates.

1. The author's parents are _____.

   a. British

   b. Indian

   c. American

2. He lives in _____.

   a. Japan

   b. Vancouver

   c. Southern California

3. The world looks like America, but America looks like the rest of the
   _____.

   a. the major cities

   b. the world

   c. North America

4. The Italian word "pizza" is _____.

   a. understood all over the world

   b. only used in Italy

   c. not used in the U.S.

5. There are many _____ people living in Brussels.

   a. Arab

   b. American

   c. global

6. When people move around the globe, so do _____.

   a. American values

   b. Americans

   c. cultural values

7. Immigrants from Asia import values to America of _____.

   a. hard work and family closeness

   b. upward mobility

   c. individualism

8. Globalization is happening very _____.

   a. slowly

   b. quickly

   c. strangely

►COMMUNICATE: Discussion

Consider how your life is affected by living in a global village. Things you buy, eat, see, hear, and touch have connections to other people, often in places far away from you!

1. Make a list of the global connections you have experienced since you woke up this morning.

Example: My alarm clock was made in Korea.
My breakfast: coffee from South America.
Listened to European pop music on the radio.
My jeans: made in Italy.
Took the bus to school—parts of the bus made in Japan.
Ate gyros (Greek) for lunch.

Your list: _____

_____

_____

_____

_____

2. Share your list in a small group.

3. Discuss the following questions:

- What are some good points of globalization?

- What are some problems of globalization?

Use the following expressions in your discussion.

Stating your Opinion	Agreeing	Disagreeing
In my opinion . . . I think . . .	I agree with you. You're right.	I disagree. I think that . . . I see your point, but . . .

➤INTERACTIVE JOURNAL RESPONSE

Choose one of the following questions and write a response. Be prepared to give an oral summary of your written response in small groups.

1. Was there anything that surprised you in this reading? Write about it.

2. What are the good points and the bad points of living in a typical village (small town)? Does living in today's "global village" share the same good and bad points? Do you like living in a global village?

TRAVEL

Travel helps us to understand the global society we live in today; instead of thinking how things may be, travel lets us see them as they are.

READING ONE

➤ BEFORE YOU BEGIN

1. Below is a list of reasons why people like to travel. Read the reasons and write one or two more reasons.

2. Now ask your classmates why they like to travel. Put a check (✓) beside the reason each classmate gives.

Reasons for travel	Classmates' Responses
1. for adventure—to try something new	_____
2. for education—to learn more history, culture	_____
3. for sightseeing—to see famous places	_____
4. _____	_____
5. _____	_____

3. Add up the checks to find the most popular reason for travel. Report your findings to the class.

➤ READING SKILL: Surveying and Predicting

Surveying, or previewing, a reading passage will help you make predictions about the content. Predicting the content before you read makes it easier to understand the reading.

Here are the steps for surveying:

a. Read the title of the reading passage.

b. Look over the reading. Read the section headings.

c. Look at any visual aids such as pictures.

➤ READING SKILL PRACTICE: Surveying and Predicting

Now use the steps for surveying to answer the following questions about Reading One.

1. What is the title of Reading One? Look up the word "safaris" if you are not sure of its meaning. From the title, what do you think this reading is about?

_____

2. Write down the section headings: _____

_____

Judging from the headings, what more can you predict about the content of the reading? Write your predictions here: _____

3. What did you learn from looking at the photograph? Explain.

_____

➤ AS YOU READ

Now read through "Experience Africa with Goliath Safaris" quickly one time.

EXPERIENCE AFRICA WITH GOLIATH SAFARIS

About Us

1   Goliath Safaris began operations in Zimbabwe, East Africa, in May 1986. We are a small family organization with a commitment to animals and   5 their habitat. Our aim is to offer our clients[1] a personal and educational safari whereby they can experience the wonders of wildlife along the Zambezi River, the fourth longest river in Africa. We will do everything possible to make   10 your trip enjoyable and satisfying. We hope that through your experience with Goliath Safaris you will take back a lasting memory of this unique African river, her traditions and her inhabitants.[2] Our operators

----

[1] *clients:* customers
[2] *inhabitants:* people or animals in a place

are all Professional River Guides licensed by the Zimbabwe National
Parks Association. We are also registered as tour operators with the   15
Zimbabwe Tourist Board.

Facilities

2   The canoes[3] are for two people. They are easy to handle, and no
prior canoeing experience is required. Canoeing instruction is given
before departure by your guide.

3   Each person is supplied with a sleeping bag, a foam mattress, and   20
a pillow. We provide one- or two-person tents with mosquito[4] netting
for those wishing to sleep under the stars, as well as canvas chairs
and tables. All this equipment is carried on board secured by safety
netting. Each person is supplied with a life jacket.

4   We provide three meals a day, together with snacks and refresh-   25
ments. Our emphasis is on tasty, healthy cooking.

Weather

5   The Zambezi Valley is warm all year round, but it can become
very hot in October through November. June through September is
considered the best time to visit the Valley. Winter (June to August)
days are usually warm, but nights can be quite cool or even cold.   30

Health

6   We recommend that you take malaria pills[5] two weeks before and
up to six weeks after your trip. A full medical kit is carried on safari,
and all our guides are licensed to give first aid.

Important

7   The river is home to crocodiles, hippos, and other hungry wildlife.
For this reason, guests are advised that swimming in the Zambezi is   35
prohibited. Walking is restricted to 50 meters away from the river by
an order from National Parks. All clients are required to sign a form
of personal responsibility before beginning their trip on the river.

8   We recommend that guests consider taking out insurance to
cover cancellation charges, for personal accident, and to cover loss   40

---

[3] *canoes:* small light boats, usually pointed at both ends, that people paddle
[4] *mosquito:* a small insect that lives in wet areas and feeds on the blood of people or animals
[5] *malaria pills:* medicine taken to guard against a dangerous disease people can get from some
  types of mosquitoes

or damage to personal possessions. We organize trips for a minimum of two persons and up to a maximum of eight. We do not offer individual trips.

What to Bring

9   Here is a basic checklist of what we suggest you bring along with you:

shorts, T-shirts	long pants, long-sleeved shirt
hat	binoculars
light blanket (winter)	camera
sunglasses	towel
raincoat or poncho	toiletries
bathing suit	flashlight
sun-protection cream	

Airport Departure Tax

10   Airport tax on departure from Zimbabwe is US $20 per person.

How to Book

11   Bookings[6] are made either directly through Goliath online or through their office in Harare. Your local travel agent can also make a booking. Your booking must be accompanied by a 10 percent deposit of the total amount of the fee.[7] Please note that reservations cannot be made without a deposit. Full fees must be paid SIX weeks prior to departure.

Cancellations

12   If a booking is cancelled 42 days prior to departure the full deposit is returned. If a booking is cancelled less than 42 days prior to departure, Goliath shall keep the full deposit and, in addition, a cancellation fee will be required as follows:

    41–29 days—40 percent of total fee
    28–14 days—60 percent of total fee
    13–0 days—100 percent of total fee

13   Please note that all cancellations must be made in writing. Cancellation insurance in the event of illness close to the date of departure is strongly recommended.

---

[6] *bookings:* travel reservations
[7] *fee:* a sum of money paid to be allowed to do something

➤ GETTING THE MAIN IDEA

Write (**T**) if the sentence is true and (**F**) if the sentence is false.

1. _____ Goliath Safaris is a professional tour organization.

2. _____ You do not have to supply your own equipment when taking a trip with Goliath Safaris.

3. _____ Goliath Safaris is not concerned about safety and health.

4. _____ A trip along the Zambezi River can be dangerous.

➤ VOCABULARY IN CONTEXT

The following sentences contain vocabulary from the brochure "Experience Africa with Goliath Safaris." Read each sentence and circle the best definition for the highlighted word.

1. He made a **commitment** to his job so he works very hard every day.

   a. promise

   b. mistake

   c. change

2. The restaurant is **unique** because it gives away free dinners every Friday night.

   a. common

   b. alone

   c. special

3. Buy your ticket **prior** to the concert because there are no tickets sold on the day of the concert.

   a. before

   b. in person

   c. on time

4. The baby was **secured** in the baby seat before they began their trip.

   a. happy

   b. damaged

   c. held safely

5. Smoking is **prohibited** in this building so you must go outside to smoke.

   a. protected

   b. not allowed

   c. praised

6. She made a **deposit** for her trip with the money she earned at her part-time job.

   a. amount of money put away

   b. something taken away

   c. plan or schedule

➤ TAKING A CLOSER LOOK

Read " Experience Africa with Goliath Safaris" again, this time focusing on details.

Circle the best answer, then underline the phrase or sentence in the reading that supports your answer. Compare your answers with a partner.

1. Goliath Safaris is a _____.

   a. government organization

   b. large company

   c. small family business

2. Equipment and supplies are carried _____.

   a. by each person

   b. by the guides

   c. in the canoes

3. If you do not know how to canoe you _____.

   a. cannot take the trip

   b. can learn before leaving

   c. need to ride with a guide

4. When is the best time to take a trip on the Zambezi?

   a. in December

   b. from November to December

   c. from June to September

5. To protect against malaria, take pills _____.

   a. only two weeks after your trip

   b. both before and after your trip

   c. before, during, and after your trip

6. Which of the following is prohibited?

   a. sleeping under the stars

   b. swimming in the Zambezi

   c. canceling your trip

7. A reservation cannot be made _____.

   a. online

   b. with a travel agent

   c. without a deposit

8. If you need to cancel your trip you must _____.

   a. call 29 days before the trip

   b. still pay for the trip

   c. write a letter of cancellation

► COMMUNICATE: Discussion

Work in pairs. Student A, read the information below. Student B, go to page 196.

Student A

1. You and your partner, (Student B), want to take a trip. Now you are deciding which country to visit—Canada or Thailand. Both of you have gathered some information on each country, but both of you are missing some information. Find out the missing information by asking Student B questions.

	Canada	Thailand
Language	English is spoken except in Quebec, where French is spoken	
Money		Thai baht, credit cards
Weather		hot all year round
Food	not spicy, lots of meat, in cities you can get food from many different countries	
Places to Visit		Buddhist temples, river boat taxis on the Chao Phraya river, the island of Koh Samui
What to Wear	blue jeans and T-shirts in summer, warm clothes and boots in winter	

Use the following questions in your conversation:

Making Conversation

- Which _____ is spoken in _____?
- How's the _____ in _____?
- What kind of _____ do people eat in _____?
- What are the best places to _____ in _____?
- What should you _____ in _____?

2. Now talk to your partner and decide which country you would like to visit.

➤ **INTERACTIVE JOURNAL RESPONSE**

Choose one of the following questions and write a response. Be prepared to give an oral summary of your written response in small groups.

1. Would you like to take a trip with Goliath Safaris? Why or why not?

2. Do you think a trip with Goliath Safaris would help you learn more about Africa? Why or why not?

3. Use the Internet to search for information on a country you would like to visit. List three pieces of information you learned from your Internet search.

4. If you were showing visitors around your country, where would you take them? Explain.

READING TWO

➤ **BEFORE YOU BEGIN**

1. What are some of the things that make your culture unique or special? For example, the type of clothing you wear, the kinds of food you eat, traditions you practice, etc. List your ideas below.

   _____   _____   _____

   _____   _____   _____

2. Why might it be difficult for a traveler on a short visit to learn and understand about the culture of your country? Share your ideas with a partner.

➤ **READING SKILL PRACTICE: Surveying and Predicting**

As you have learned, surveying or previewing a reading passage will help you make predictions. Survey the poem in Reading Two to help you predict the content.

1. Read the title of the poem. What do you think it means?

   _____

2. Skim the poem looking for italicized words, special punctuation, and format style. Write down what you found. _____

   _____

3. Skim the first and last stanza of the poem. Now try to predict what the poem is about. Circle one of the following:

It's about _____

    a. traveler who cannot see out the car window.

    b. the lack of understanding between the traveler and the local people.

    c. what local people do when they see travelers in a car.

4. What additional information can you gather from the picture? Explain.

► **LISTENING FOCUS**

Listen while your teacher reads the poem "A World of Difference" for the first time.

Now listen again and answer the following questions. Compare your answers with your classmates.

    a. WHO are the main characters of the poem?

    b. WHERE are they?

    c. WHAT are they doing?

A WORLD OF DIFFERENCE
Anonymous (Bhutan) (from *Contours*)

1   Our eyes met
    And for a few seconds
    . . . two worlds apart
    Faced each other.

2   Standing with a pick[1] in her hand,   5
    A sleeping baby on her back,
    She stopped work for a few minutes.

3   Headscarf of faded cloth,
    Tied back dusty, uncombed hair.
    Hands and feet leathered   10

---

[1] *pick:* a tool which is used to break up hard ground or stones

From constant work on
The mountain road.

4   Snow lay around the shacks[2] . . .
A child playing, no nappy,[3] no shoes.
Icicles hanging on bamboo walls.   15
A group crouched[4] around a wood fire
Turn . . .
And met our gaze too.

5   What do you really think of us?
Foreigners?   20
Strangers?
From another planet . . .
Called "*Affluence*";
As we pass by over your handiwork,
Your toil and sweat.   25

6   She stared back at me.
How could I understand?
Not just a car window
Between us
. . . A world of difference.   30

---

[2] *shack:* small, poorly put together house
[3] *nappy:* diaper made of cloth or paper
[4] *to crouch:* to half-sit, half-stand close to the ground

➤ GETTING THE MAIN IDEA

Look at your answer to number 3 of Reading Skill Practice. Do you still agree with your answer?

➤ VOCABULARY STUDY

The following sentences contain vocabulary from the poem "A World of Difference." Circle the best definition for the highlighted word.

1. His T-shirt was **faded** from working in the fields under the strong sunlight.
   a. new
   b. losing its color
   c. old

2. The air was **dusty** because there were so many cars driving on the old road.
   a. dirty
   b. clean
   c. fresh

3. There was **constant** noise from the machine, which kept going all night long.
   a. welcome
   b. black
   c. never ending

4. We could recognize their **affluence** by all the money they spent while on vacation.
   a. richness
   b. poverty
   c. answer

5. The farmers would **toil** in the fields day after day so there would be enough food for their families.
   a. drive
   b. work
   c. dance

➤ TAKING A CLOSER LOOK

Read "A World of Difference" again, this time focusing on details.

Decide if the following sentences are true (**T**) or false (**F**), then go back to the poem and underline the phrase or sentence that supports your answer. Compare your answers with your classmates.

1. _____ The woman in the poem did not make eye contact with the traveler.

2. _____ The woman in the poem worked hard.

3. _____ The child in the poem was warmly dressed.

4. _____ The walls where the woman lived were made of brick.

5. _____ The traveler in the car called the woman and her family "Foreigners," "Strangers."

6. _____ Travelers spend a long time looking at the local handiwork.

7. _____ The traveler feels some difference between his/her life and the life of the local woman.

 ## ➤ COMMUNICATE: Exchanging Information

Work with a partner. You are going to read about one student's summer travel experience. Your partner is going to read about another student's summer travel experience. Your teacher will tell you if you are Student A or Student B.

1. First, read about your student's summer travel experience. Student A, read about Pat (a woman) on Page 25. Student B, read about Terry (a man) on page 196.

2. Then go through the following questions with your partner. Tell your partner about your student's travel experiences.

   a. Where did the student go?

   b. What did the student do?

   c. What did the student learn from the experience?

Use the following expressions in your discussion.

Stating your Opinion	Agreeing	Disagreeing
I think . . . because . . .	I agree because . . .	I disagree. In my opinion . . .

3. Which student do you think had the best travel experience? Why?

Student A

Pat wrote:

"I traveled to a small village in Mexico this past summer and had a chance to meet a Mexican farming family. I was lucky enough to be able to stay with them for a few days. It gave me a real chance to see how many Mexicans live. I even got to join in on one of their summer festivals and to learn how to cook some traditional Mexican food. It was a great opportunity for me to experience the culture firsthand and to realize how important the family is in Mexican culture."

➤ INTERACTIVE JOURNAL RESPONSE

Choose one of the following questions and write a response. Be prepared to give an oral summary of your written response in small groups.

1. Read stanza 5 of the poem one more time. In this stanza the traveler asks, "What do you really think of us?" Imagine you are the local woman. What would be her reply?

2. Do you think traveling will help you better understand the global society you live in today? Why or why not?

3. How can we best learn about the people and culture of a country when we travel?

BIODIVERSITY

Scientists estimate that there are about 14 million species (kinds) of animals and plants on Earth. "Biodiversity" means this rich variety of species. The loss of biodiversity is a serious global problem today: For example, we are losing about 100 species a day because tropical rain forests are being cut down. Whose problem is biodiversity loss? In the global village we live in, it is everybody's problem.

READING ONE

➤ BEFORE YOU BEGIN

Take the quiz to see how much you know about biodiversity.

How Much Do You Know About Biodiversity?

Write (**T**) in front of each statement you believe is true, and (**F**) in front of each statement you believe is false.

1. _____ Pollution will be the greatest cause of the loss of species in the next 50 years.

2. _____ We know the value of most plants and animals.

3. _____ Humans live by eating about 10,000 different plant species.

4. _____ Twenty percent of the world's species are found in the tropical rainforests.

5. _____ Global warming is affected by biodiversity.

Now survey the article and make some predictions: Why do you suppose biodiversity is important? _____

➤ AS YOU READ

Read the article more carefully to see if your predictions were correct.

THE IMPORTANCE OF BIODIVERSITY
by Steve Barnes from *Trees for Life*

1   The major areas of biodiversity in the world are now endangered. More than half the world's species are found in tropical rainforests like the Amazon. Deforestation of these areas will be the greatest cause of the loss of species in the next 50 years. At current rates, it is estimated that 5 to 10 percent of tropical forest species will be lost   5 per decade—roughly 100 species a day. This loss of biodiversity is one of the greatest problems facing us today. There are many reasons why it is important to preserve biodiversity. Some say we should save

species for their own sake.[1] Perhaps the most important reason is for human survival.   10

2   The real value of the roughly 14 million plant and animal species to humans is still unknown. Losing species, even snakes and spiders, might matter for a number of reasons. History shows that even species that seem insignificant can make important contributions. Today's apparently useless species may contain tomorrow's medicine.   15 For example, the drug penicillin was developed from simple bread mold.[2] The medicine for malaria, quinine, comes from the cinchona tree. Scientists have learned that over 1300 rainforest plants in the Amazon have medicinal value. But only one plant species in a hundred has been tested for possible applications for human health. At   20 the National Cancer Institute in the United States, a new program has been started to test plants from all over the world for their possible effects on cancer and AIDS.

3   Besides being a source of medicine, biodiversity is also important for agriculture. Many varieties of food are already being lost: In the   25 past 40 years, 95 percent of the native wheat varieties in Greece have disappeared. Today's modern agriculture depends on a dangerously narrow variety of species. Roughly 92 percent of the world's rice is grown in Asia but only a few species. A disease or insect that affects one of these rice species could have a terrible impact on world food   30 security. The Irish potato famine in the nineteenth century was devastating because only a few varieties of potato were grown in Ireland and all of these caught the same disease. Diversity reduces these risks. It also provides agricultural scientists with the material for breeding[3] stronger species. Cross-breeding domestic plants with   35 wild ones can improve yields[4] and produce new types that are stronger against diseases and insects.

4   As for diet and health, throughout history it is estimated that human beings have used more than 10,000 edible plant species, but now barely 150 are grown for the human diet. Most people live off   40 no more than 12 species. Doctors recommend a much wider variety of food for good health.

---

[1] *for their own sake:* in order to please or honor them
[2] *mold:* a green growth of fungus on things that sit in warm, wet air.
[3] *breeding:* producing, bringing up
[4] *yields:* the amount produced (in this case, plants)

5   There are two other reasons for preserving biodiversity, both connected to global warming.[5] First, when tropical rainforests are burned or cut, large amounts of carbon dioxide are released. This makes global warming worse. We need to keep biodiverse areas to keep our climate in balance. Second, as a result of climate change in the future caused by global warming, many food species will die. Food species' diversity will be important for human food production in a changing environment. In fact, biodiversity may be crucial for providing plant species that can grow in different climates.

6   Some loss of species is perhaps inevitable—the history of life on Earth shows this. This does not mean, however, that the rich biodiversity of our planet should not be protected. Possible methods range from high-tech operations in genetic engineering[6] to simply the preservation of rainforests and the encouragement of biodiversity in agriculture and diet. Maintaining biodiversity is important for our present and future well-being, and perhaps our survival.

---

[5] *global warming:* worldwide climate change (getting warmer) believed to be caused by too much C02 from the burning of fossil fuels

[6] *genetic engineering:* the science of manipulating the biology of a species to improve it

➤ GETTING THE MAIN IDEA

What is the reading about? Check the best statement. Compare your answer with your classmates.

1. _____ We must preserve a diversity of species for their own sake.

2. _____ We must preserve a diversity of species for the well-being of humans.

3. _____ We must preserve a diversity of species for food.

➤ READING SKILL: Vocabulary in Context

One of the most important reading skills you can develop is guessing the meaning of unknown words rather than using your dictionary. Often students will reach for their dictionary as soon as they see any unknown word, or they will ask the teacher or another student. But you can develop your reading skills by using the words and sentences around the unknown word to guess what it means. By doing this, you will improve your reading pace and also your comprehension.

► READING SKILL PRACTICE: Guessing from Context

Use the context—the other words in the sentence —to help you to guess the meaning of an unknown word. For example, try to guess what "insignificant" means in the following sentence from Reading One:

History shows that even species that seem **insignificant** can make important contributions.

> **a.** important
>
> **b.** unimportant
>
> **c.** expensive

From the key words "even," "seem," and "important," you probably concluded that the word "insignificant" means "unimportant."

Part A

Below, there are two sentences using each unknown word—one from the reading, the other an extra example. Without a dictionary, use the context of the sentences to determine the meaning of the highlighted word. From your guess, circle the best definition for the highlighted word.

1. With more than half the world's species found in tropical rainforests like the Amazon, **deforestation** will be the greatest cause of the loss of species in the next 50 years.

    After **deforestation**, the land was dry, dusty, and bare.

    > **a.** the act of cutting the forest down
    >
    > **b.** the act of planting new trees
    >
    > **c.** the act of setting up fire stations.

2. There are many reasons why it is important to **preserve** biodiversity.

    To **preserve** her beauty, she wore a sun hat and used expensive skin creams.

    > **a.** destroy
    >
    > **b.** keep, save
    >
    > **c.** hide

3. Today's **apparently** useless species may contain tomorrow's medicine.

   Apparently, the room was empty, but when he turned on the light, people jumped up and shouted, "Surprise!"

   a. friendly

   b. without any doubt

   c. seemingly

4. A disease or insect that affects one of these rice species could have a terrible **impact** on world food security.

   The movie had such an **impact** on her that she remembered it forever.

   a. effect

   b. expense

   c. secret

5. The Irish potato famine in the nineteenth century was **devastating** because only a few varieties of potato were grown in Ireland and all of these caught the same disease.

   The **devastating** fire caused many people to become homeless.

   a. destroying completely

   b. harming a little

   c. uncomfortable

Part B

Guess the meaning of the highlighted word from the context of the two sentences. Write a definition or a synonym. Then compare your work with another student. Finally, use a dictionary to check your accuracy.

6. Cross-breeding **domestic** plants with wild ones can improve yields and produce new types that are stronger against diseases and insects.

   Domestic cats are much smaller than lions or tigers.

   Your explanation: _____

   Dictionary: _____

7. In fact, biodiversity may be **crucial** for providing species that can grow in different climates.

It is **crucial** for you to drink water when the weather is so hot.

Your explanation: _____

Dictionary: _____

8. Some loss of species is perhaps **inevitable**—the history of life on Earth shows this.

It is **inevitable** that we will die someday.

Your explanation: _____

Dictionary: _____

9. **Maintaining** biodiversity is important for our present and future well-being, and perhaps our survival.

To **maintain** the garden's beauty, they watered it every day and took good care of it.

Your explanation: _____

Dictionary: _____

➤ TAKING A CLOSER LOOK

Go back to the Quiz on page 28, and find the answers to those questions in the reading. Underline the phrase or sentence in the reading that supports your answer. Then compare with a partner.

➤ COMMUNICATE: Values Clarification

On page 34 is a list of reasons to preserve biodiversity. According to your point of view, rank the reasons from 1 (most important) to 7 (least important). Then share your ranking with three or four students and try to reach a group consensus. Present your group's final rankings to the class.

Reasons to preserve biodiversity

_____ To protect possible medicine sources, for example, for cancer or AIDS treatment.

_____ To protect world food security against the risk of disease or pests.

_____ To provide a wider variety of food species for people's diet and health.

_____ To keep the climate in balance.

_____ To provide a variety of species that can cope with new climate conditions in the future.

_____ To respect nature.

_____ To preserve plant and animal species for their own sake.

Use the following expressions in your discussion.

Asking an Opinion	Agreeing	Disagreeing
Which one did you rank number 1?	That's right.	Yes, but don't you think . . . ?
How about you?	I think so, too.	That's true, but . . . .

➤ INTERACTIVE JOURNAL RESPONSE

Choose one of the following questions and write a response. Be prepared to give an oral summary of your written response in small groups.

1. Do you agree with the writer of this article that the loss of biodiversity is one of the world's most serious problems? Explain.

2. Recently, environmental groups have shown concern about endangered animal species: certain species of whales, the panda, the snow leopard, and so forth. Name one animal that is endangered in your country. What is your response to endangered species: Do you think we should try to protect and save them? Why or why not?

3. What can we do as individuals to support biodiversity?

READING TWO

➤ BEFORE YOU BEGIN

Imagine you order your lunch at your favorite fast food restaurant. What does each food item contain? Make a list like the one below (Contents). Then compare lists with a partner. Finally, try to identify the source of each food item.

Example

Food Item	Contents	Possible Source
hamburger	beef	South America
	bread	wheat from Canada
	lettuce	local farms
	tomato	local farms

➤ AS YOU READ

Read the following article through quickly to get an idea of what the reading is about.

DIVERSITY IN DIET HELPS PRESERVE SPECIES
by Meriel Hiramoto (from *Asahi Evening News*)

1   One of the most difficult environmental tasks is trying to preserve at least some of the 14 million species on the planet. The simplest thing we can do to support biodiversity is to eat sensibly. The plants and animals that we eat show our relationship with nature and bind

us to her. The greater the diversity we maintain in our diet, the   5
greater the diversity we nurture[1] in the fields and the oceans.

2   Fast food is a wonderful and a terrible phenomenon.[2] It is indeed
fast; it is also easy to carry out, hygienic,[3] and familiar. On the other
hand, it is environmentally devastating, inadequate in meeting our
daily requirements for nutrition,[4] and reduces biodiversity. Fast food   10
chains often raise beef in rainforests. Rainforests are cleared for cows
to live on. As a result, a medium-size hamburger represents approximately five square meters of rainforests and all the hundreds and
thousands of species that had lived on that five square meters. The
land beneath rainforests is not good for cows to stay on a long time.   15
It soon becomes dry and bare, and has to be abandoned within a couple of years and the whole process repeated somewhere else. It
already takes a lot of rainforests to keep hamburger eaters happy in
Japan and America. It will take even more to keep them happy in
China, Vietnam, and all the other countries opening their wallets to   20
multinational fast food companies.

3   The other problem with fast food is that it relies on a narrow range
of food types. This affects agriculture. Fast food chains serve the same
food all over the world. That means they serve the same french fries
made from the same type of potatoes and the same salads made from   25
the same type of lettuce and tomatoes in every country. Fast food chains
move into countries where the fast food ingredients are quite different
from traditional local ingredients. Local farmers abandon their
traditional crops and try to grow the food needed for the very limited
international menus. This reduces the diversity of local crops.   30

4   So, if fast food reduces biodiversity, perhaps you will decide to eat
at home. How about the food at your local supermarket?
Supermarkets appear to have a huge diversity of fruits, vegetables, and
meats to choose from. Indeed, in many developed countries a large
supermarket will have an average of 22,000 items. The diversity,   35
however, is only in the packaging. The content is pretty much all the
same. Nearly everything that you can buy to eat at a supermarket
comes from only 30 plants and six animals. We are being forced to rely
on fewer and fewer varieties of plants and animals. Why is this? These

---

[1] *to nurture:* to grow something, to take care of
[2] *phenomenon:* a fact, thing, or happening
[3] *hygienic:* clean and free from disease
[4] *nutrition:* what people need from food to stay healthy

days, food is produced by the system of farming called "monoculture." Instead of a small farm producing a diverse variety of crops, large farms produce only one type of plant or animal. This is easier and more profitable for the farmer, and cheaper for the customer. But as a result, our food choices are being dangerously narrowed simply for convenience. The biodiversity in our diet is getting smaller.

5 What can we do? As individuals, we can nurture biodiversity by shopping in season, buying organic[5] produce, and favoring less common types of food. Here are some examples:

Normal Choice	Biodiversity-friendly choice
White eggs. Virtually all white eggs come from white Leghorn chickens.	Brown eggs—preferably free range.
Regular milk, 95 percent of which comes from Holstein cows.	Jersey or Guernsey milk—preferably hormone free.
Wheat bread.	Multigrain, rye, barley, oat, corn bread. Bagels and tortillas, preferably organic.
White rice.	Brown rice, barley, millet. Preferably organic.
Potatoes—mainly russet.	New potatoes, sweet potatoes, taro, pumpkin—definitely organic since they absorb more chemicals than any other vegetables.
Soft drinks (soda).	Fresh fruit and vegetable juices.

6 We try to simplify our lives. We try to simplify nature. The trouble is that our own bodies and the world around us need biodiversity.

---

[5] *organic:* grown naturally without chemicals

➤ GETTING THE MAIN IDEA

What is the reading about? Check one. Then compare your answer with your classmates.

1. _____ Eating the same type of food every day reduces biodiversity of agriculture, which may endanger future food sources.

2. _____ Because fast food is not healthy, we should eat other types of food including brown rice and brown eggs.

3. _____ Supermarkets do not encourage biodiversity.

➤ READING SKILL: Using Grammar to Guess Meaning

Another way you can guess the meaning of unknown words is to use the grammar of the sentence to identify the function of the word. Is the unknown word a noun, verb, pronoun, adjective, or adverb? This will help you to guess the meaning of the word more easily.

Example: One of the most difficult environmental **tasks** is trying to preserve at least some of the 14 million species on the planet.

What is the part of speech of **task** in this sentence? What do you suppose **task** means?

Task is a noun and it means "a job," "a piece of work," "something to be done."

➤ READING SKILL PRACTICE: Using Grammar to Guess Meaning

Guess the meaning of the highlighted word from the grammatical context of the sentence. First, decide what part of speech the unknown word is (verb, noun, adjective, adverb). Next, try to guess its meaning. Then compare your idea with another student. Finally, use a dictionary to check your answer.

1. The plants and animals we eat show our relationship with nature and **bind** us to her.

   Part of speech: _____

   Your guess about the meaning: _____

   Dictionary meaning: _____

2. Fast food is **inadequate** in meeting our daily requirements for nutrition.

   Part of speech: _____

   Your guess about the meaning: _____

   Dictionary meaning: _____

3. The land soon becomes dry and bare and has to be **abandoned** in a couple of years.

   Part of speech: _____

   Your guess about the meaning: _____

   Dictionary meaning: _____

4. Local farmers abandon their traditional **crops** and try to grow the food needed the fast food restaurants.

   Part of speech: _____

   Your guess about the meaning: _____

   Dictionary meaning: _____

5. This is easier and more **profitable** for the farmer, and cheaper for the customer.

   Part of speech: _____

   Your guess about the meaning: _____

   Dictionary meaning: _____

6. We should buy organic potatoes and pumpkins because they **absorb** more chemicals than any other vegetables.

   Part of speech: _____

   Your guess about the meaning: _____

   Dictionary meaning: _____

➤ TAKING A CLOSER LOOK

Read the passage again, this time looking for details. Decide if the following sentences are true (**T**) or false (**F**). Go back to the reading and underline the phrase or sentence that supports your answer. Then compare your answers with your classmates.

1. _____ The author believes that by eating a diverse diet, we can support biodiversity.

2. _____ Fast food is unfamiliar and unhygienic.

3. _____ Beef for fast food hamburgers is often raised on cleared rainforest land.

4. _____ Local farmers can make more money from their traditional crops than from monocrops for fast food.

5. _____ Supermarkets have a wide variety of vegetables and meats.

6. _____ The author thinks that "simple is best."

➤ COMMUNICATE: Presenting Research

1. Interview your parents, grandparents, elderly relatives or neighbors, or teachers about their childhood food. Ask them the following questions.

   a. Did they have the same variety of foods that you have?

   b. What did they eat for their regular daily meals? Was that food indigenous (native to their country), introduced from overseas, or imported?

   c. What were their special foods for holidays?

2. Share your research with a small group. Together, make a summary of the group's research and present it to the class. Use the following expressions in your discussion.

Asking for Information	Responding to Information	Sharing Information
What did your research show?	Really?	As far as my interview shows . . .
What did you find?	Me too.	From my interview, it seems . . .

➤INTERACTIVE JOURNAL RESPONSE

Choose one of the following questions and write a response. Be prepared to give an oral summary of your written response in small groups.

1. "The greater the diversity we maintain in our diet, the greater the diversity we nurture in the fields and the oceans." What does the writer mean? Explain in your own words.

2. If you could design the weekly lunch menu for a restaurant, what would the menu choices be? Why? (Reasons might involve taste, cost, nutrition, biodiversity, pollution, and so forth.)

3. Based on your interview, write about how daily diet has changed over the years. How does the food of your interviewee compare with your daily diet? What are your conclusions about the interview?

4. Would changing our diet make a difference to the earth? Why or why not?

LOVE

Recently the concept of finding love and romance has changed in many ways. Due to the Internet, the traditional "love at first sight" has become "love at first byte" for many people seeking romance around the world.

READING ONE

➤ BEFORE YOU BEGIN

Work with a partner. Answer yes or no to the following questions. Then ask your partner the questions. Give reasons for your answers.

Questions	Reasons	Your Partner's Reasons
Do you believe in love at first sight?		
Would you ever go on a blind date?		
Would you ever try using a match-maker to find a partner?		
Do you think it's important to be in love before you get married?		

➤ READING SKILL: Identifying the Topic of a Reading

The topic is the subject matter of a reading. The topic is expressed in a word or phrase, never in a sentence. The easiest way to identify the topic is to ask yourself, "What or who is it about?" The answer will be the topic. The easiest way to identify the topic of a reading is to skim the contents before beginning to read.

➤ READING SKILL PRACTICE: Identifying the Topic of a Reading

Work with a partner.

1. Read the title. Look up the word "courtship" in your dictionary if you are not sure of its meaning. Explain what you think the title means.

2. Skim the reading. Read the words in quotation marks and words followed by colons. Finally, read the first and last sentence of the reading. Based on your skimming, which of the following best describes the contents of the reading?

   a._____ how men and women fall in love around the world

   b._____ how falling in love is different around the world

   c._____ the reasons men and women fall in love around the world

➤ **AS YOU READ**

Now read through "Romantic Love" quickly one time. As you read, ask yourself, "What is the topic?"

ROMANTIC LOVE: THE BASICS OF COURTSHIP
from "The Basics of Flirting," www.search.wesleyan.edu:/query

1   "Falling in love" is universal, but the belief that it is an essential part of marriage is not. Only a few areas such as the United States, Canada, Western Europe, and Polynesia have a traditional belief that falling in love is a desirable and necessary requirement for marriage. Other cultures, especially in Asia and some parts of Europe,   5 have tended to separate romance from marriage in the past. In Japan, for example, the practice of omiai or "arranged marriage" has been the traditional approach of finding a marriage partner. These days, however, it seems that even in the most traditional societies around the world "falling in love" is on the rise. So exactly how do two   10 people carry out this Western-Polynesian tradition of romantic courtship?

2   Numerous research studies in interpersonal behavior confirm there is a universal sequence[1] of behavioral steps by which two people are attracted to each other, and get closer. Although this sequence can also   15 be observed in studies of animal behavior, and many elements are common across cultures, the following elements of flirtation[2] describe behaviors that are mainly related to Western culture. The following "Core Courtship Sequence" describes the series of behaviors made

---

[1] *sequence:* a group of things that happen in order
[2] *flirtation:* the act of flirting: smiling and talking in a way that attracts the attention of the opposite sex

by either a woman or a man, which represent progressive closeness   20
and acceptance. These behaviors involve recognizing the personal
"boundaries" of the other person—the physical and emotional space
that a person needs—and then knowing how and when to get closer.
There are six steps in the sequence.

3   The Approach: One person approaches the other or moves to be   25
closer physically to another person. Example: A woman sits down
next to a man in a coffee shop or a man stands near a woman in
a dance club.

4   The Behavioral Acknowledgement: The person who has been
approached uses some subtle body language to show they recognize   30
and accept the other person's presence. Example: He or she simply
may look up, move over to make room, nod slightly, or signal with
a glancing eye contact.

5   The Mild Verbal Acknowledgement: The two people may then strike
up[3] a conversation with each other. They might talk about impersonal   35
matters such as the weather. At this point, the verbal exchange is not
for the purpose of sharing a valuable insight about life, it is just a way
to further the developing contact. Examples: Verbal acknowledgements
might include "please pass the ketchup" to "have you seen the
waitress?" to "that dress you're wearing looks great on you."   40

6   Physical Orientation: Over a period of time, a couple that has
begun to talk may also begin to orient themselves physically to one
another, to turn toward one another until they are fully facing one
another. It can take minutes or hours . . . or weeks or months . . . for
this step to happen. Without this physical orientation towards one   45
another, not much can happen.

7   Touching: The woman or the man touches the other briefly. Any
heavy or sudden gestures at this point could affect the progress of the
relationship between the two people or even cause the sequence to
stop. Example: A couple might brush their hands against one anoth-   50
er while reaching for a drink by accident, or the woman might pat
the man on the arm in the middle of a shared joke.

8   Synchrony:[4] If all goes well to this point, a couple may begin to
move in synchrony with one another. Example: When talking the

---

[3] *strike up:* begin
[4] *synchrony:* things happening at the same time

couple might move their hands or their heads in the same way or at   55
the same time. The couple may feel at ease[5] with each other and may
begin to feel a strong attraction to one another by this point in the
courtship sequence. The signals flowing back and forth between the
two people are a measure of what some people refer to as "physical
chemistry." At this point, the courtship sequence can be said to have   60
successfully developed into the possibility of a romantic relationship.

---

[5] *feel at ease:* feel comfortable

►READING SKILL: Identifying the Topic of Each Paragraph

Recognizing the topic of each paragraph while you read is the next step in helping you identify the topic of a whole reading passage. The information you gather about each paragraph can help you identify the topic with more accuracy.

►READING SKILL PRACTICE: Identifying the Topic of Each Paragraph

1. Read the topics below. You will find one topic for each paragraph in Reading One. Next read each paragraph and match it with one of the topics. Compare your answers with a partner. The first one is done for you.

   a. _paragraph 8_ how two people show their ease with one another

   b. _____ the concept of falling in love as a cultural trend worldwide

   c. _____ how two people orient themselves to one another

   d. _____ an introduction to the elements of flirting

   e. _____ the first physical interaction

   f. _____ the meeting stage

   g. _____ the small-talk stage

   h. _____ the nonverbal interaction stage

2. What is the topic of this reading? Check back to your answer in question 2 of "Reading Skill Practice." Do you agree with your first choice? If not, make a new choice. Then discuss your answer with your classmates.

➤ VOCABULARY IN CONTEXT

Find each word or phrase in the paragraph indicated in brackets [ ]. From the context, guess the meaning. Then match the definitions in column B with the vocabulary in column A. The first one has been done for you.

	A		B
1. _b_	universal [1]	a.	not noticeable
2. _____	interpersonal [2]	b.	worldwide
3. _____	acknowledgement [4]	c.	an understanding about something
4. _____	subtle [4]	d.	to face in a certain direction
5. _____	impersonal [5]	e.	relationship between two people
6. _____	insight [5]	f.	to recognize
7. _____	orientation [6]	g.	something unrelated to the person

➤ TAKING A CLOSER LOOK

Read "Falling In Love," this time focusing on details. Decide if the following sentences are true (T) or false (F). Go back to the reading and underline the sentence or phrase that supports your answer. Then compare your answers with your classmates.

1. _____ Falling in love is recognized worldwide.

2. _____ In Japan the tradition is for couples to meet by chance just as they do in Western societies.

3. _____ Personal "boundaries" means the physical and emotional space that exists between two people.

4. _____ A man always approaches a woman first in a courtship sequence.

5. _____ Couples usually touch each other before they speak to one another in a courtship sequence.

6. _____ The step of physical orientation takes only one minute.

7. _____ Synchrony means movement in the opposite direction to the other person.

8. _____ If there is "physical chemistry" between two people it means they are attracted to each other.

➤ COMMUNICATE: Role Play

Work with a partner. Read the following situation then write a short role play based on the courtship sequence from Reading One.

Use some of the following phrases in your the role play.

Hi, mind if I …?	Please …
My name's …	Nice to meet you. My name's …
Would you mind …	Oh, no …
The weather's really …	Yes, I think …

Student A

You are sitting in a crowded coffee shop. You notice an attractive person standing holding a cup of coffee, waiting to find a seat. Just by chance someone leaves the seat next to you. You would really like to get to know the person holding the coffee. What do you do? What do you say?

Student B

You have just paid for your coffee and would like to find a seat so you can relax and drink it. As you look around the coffee shop, you spot an attractive person sitting by an empty seat. It looks like a good chance to sit down and relax and maybe even meet someone interesting. What do you do? What do you say?

➤ INTERACTIVE JOURNAL RESPONSE

Choose one of the following questions and write a response. Be prepared to give an oral summary of your written response in small groups.

1. What is the traditional approach to finding a marriage partner in your culture?

2. Do you think young people today still flirt in the traditional way described in the reading? Explain.

3. Do you think love and marriage are different? Explain your ideas.

READING TWO

➤ BEFORE YOU BEGIN

Work with a partner.

1. What are some of the different ways people "fall in love" or find a marriage partner besides the traditional courtship sequence?

   Example: a. <u>put an advertisement in the newspaper</u>

   b. _____

   c. _____

   d. _____

2. Which way do you think might work best? Explain.

➤ READING SKILL PRACTICE: Identifying the Topic

1. Read the title. From the title, predict where courtship takes place in this reading.

2. Skim the reading. Notice words in italics and in quotation marks. Then quickly read the first and last paragraphs of the reading. Based on your skimming, what do you think this reading will be about?

   It's going to be about _____

➤ AS YOU READ

Now read through "Cybercourtship" quickly one time. As you read, ask yourself, "What is the topic?"

CYBERCOURTSHIP

1   It is hard to imagine the basic human behavior called "flirting" ever changing significantly. Yet recently, there has been a strange new twist put on romantic courtship. It is called "cybercourtship." 5

2   Internet technology has now made it possible for more people to meet and, in some cases, develop a romance online. There are numerous chat rooms, bulletin boards, online dating services and personal–ad posting services 10 available on the World Wide Web—which some are discovering is a virtual meeting ground for couples. If you're shy, meeting online can be a much less frightening experience than meeting in person for the first time. And if you're busy, you can e-mail and develop an online relationship at your convenience. These days, the Internet allows 15 users to meet in virtual reality and communicate the process of first love without going through those awkward[1] moments in the traditional face-to-face flirtation sequence.

3   Traditionally, humans have recognized their growing attraction for other people via stages of *physical* proximity. Except for maybe 20 the platonic[2] relationship that one might develop with a pen pal, it is natural that you want to see and know the other person before developing any genuine desire for that person. But Internet social life demonstrates that it is not necessary to see someone in order to begin to feel something for that person. Sometimes it is easier to get to 25 know someone because online there are fewer of the inhibitions[3] that normally go with visual contact.

4   With virtual romance there is no chaperone.[4] The boundaries between people's thoughts quickly become very "permeable," that is, easy to pass or flow through. People say things to one another online 30 that they would never mention to a new acquaintance at a party or in a bar. It can be easy to form a quick, intense bond online. This

---

[1] *awkward:* uncomfortable

[2] *platonic:* a friendly, nonphysical relationship with someone

[3] *inhibitions:* feelings of shyness or fear that make it difficult for a person to act naturally

[4] *chaperone:* an older person (usually a woman) who accompanies a single female on social occasions

does not happen simply because the inhibitions of physical proximity are removed. Talking (writing) online has its own characteristics of freedom and speed—grammar and syntax rules no longer apply as they do in formal writing or even in speaking, and words therefore flow much faster and more expressively. It seems to be so free, completely without boundaries or rules. But is it?

5   Although informational boundaries and government controls are certainly decreased through the Internet, strangely enough there still exist subtle interpersonal boundaries. In fact, although Internet communications technology has made some boundaries more permeable than they were before and allows us to make certain kinds of direct connections much faster, it has actually made the boundaries much more sensitive and difficult to predict. Anyone who has used e-mail much has noticed how easily one's casual, quickly typed comment can be misunderstood, how suddenly the tone of e-mails can change, how small conflicts can develop rapidly from a few lines. That is, in cyberspace, because of the lack of physical cues and feedback, it is much easier to misunderstand, upset, and insult the receiver, and likewise, become bothered by the message. Because communication happens very quickly and is based solely on written words without any physical feedback from body language, it becomes hard to control the interaction. In short, flirtation and courtship in cyberspace often require more, not less, sophistication in approaching complex interpersonal boundaries.

6   "Oh, I think I'm in love. This woman I met online writes the most beautiful things. I look forward to each e-mail. We are going to arrange to meet soon, and I'm so excited about it. But . . . I have this fear that she will be a disappointment in person," writes one Internet romance seeker. Well yes, she may indeed be a disappointment, maybe even a disaster! You may be a disappointment to her, too. Too many singles seeking partners online have mistakenly concluded that cyberspace connections mean "real love," without all the difficult effort of the actual relationship. But eventually we have to face the real, physical person in order to complete the courtship sequence toward marriage.

➤ READING SKILL PRACTICE: Identifying the Topic

1. Read the topics below. You will find one topic for each paragraph in Reading Two. Re-read each of the paragraphs. Then match each paragraph with one of the topics. Finally, compare your answers with a partner.

   a. __paragraph 2__ reasons for virtual courtship

   b. _____ cybercourtship defined as a new type of romance

   c. _____ realities of cybercourtship

   d. _____ the freedom of cybercourtship

   e. _____ why virtual romance may be easier

   f. _____ problems related to virtual romance

2. What is the topic of this reading? Based on the information you have gathered, discuss with your partner what you think is the topic of this reading. Then write the topic in the space below.

   _____

3. Write your topic on the blackboard. Now discuss all the topics with your teacher and then decide which one you think is the best topic for this reading.

➤ VOCABULARY IN CONTEXT

Find each word or phrase in the paragraph indicated in brackets [ ]. From the context, guess the meaning. Then circle the best definition.

1. convenience [2]   a. quickness   b. ease

2. proximity [3]   a. closeness   b. frequency

3. boundaries [4]   a. limits   b. edges

4. sensitive [5]   a. delicate   b. hard

5. insult [5]   a. to praise someone   b. to hurt another's feelings

➤ TAKING A CLOSER LOOK

Read "Cybercourtship" again, this time focusing on details. Decide if the following sentences are true (**T**) or false (**F**). Go back to the reading and underline the sentence or phrase that supports your answer. Then compare your answers with your classmates.

1. _____ Internet courtship offers a type of romance.

2. _____ Chat rooms are places where people can meet face-to-face.

3. _____ Online courtship is sometimes easier for people than courtship in the real world.

4. _____ With the Internet, you can actually begin to like someone before meeting the person.

5. _____ Face-to-face relationships develop more quickly compared to online relationships.

6. _____ Expressing feelings online is easier than in public because there is no one to watch over you online.

7. _____ The lack of body language can make it easier for two people to communicate online.

8. _____ In the end, the success of cybercourtship depends on real face-to-face interaction.

► COMMUNICATE: Interview

Work in a small group.

Online forums such as chat rooms and bulletin boards are not only for online romance. There are many other reasons for using online forums. Interview your group members to find out their ideas. Then write them in the chart that follows. Follow the example.

Group Member	What is the best reason for using online forums?
Joe	Chat rooms let people who have the same interests communicate.

Use the following phrases in your interviews with group members.

Interviewing	Stating an Opinion
What do you think about ...?	Well, I think ...
Do you think chat rooms ...?	In my opinion ...
So how about ...?	It seems to me that ...

➤INTERACTIVE JOURNAL RESPONSE

Choose one of the following questions and write a response. Be prepared to give an oral summary of your written response in small groups.

1. What do you think about finding romance on the Internet?

2. The author says that e-mail messages can be misinterpreted because of the lack of physical cues and feedback (see paragraph 5). Can you think of a time when your message was misinterpreted or a time when you misinterpreted someone else's message? Explain what happened. In your opinion, what is the best way to avoid a misunderstanding through e-mail messages?

3. What are the good points of cybercourtship? What are the problems of cybercourtship?

TIME

Time is so basic in the human experience that we often take it for granted. Yet individuals and cultures experience time in

READING ONE

➤ BEFORE YOU BEGIN

1. There are many expressions in English using the word "time." Match the following idioms with their meanings:

Idioms	Meanings
_____ Time flies.	**a.** I had a wonderful experience.
_____ Time will tell.	**b.** We will find out the truth in the future.
_____ Time is the great healer.	**c.** Time seems to pass quickly.
_____ I had the time of my life.	**d.** Things will mend naturally with time.

Can you think of any other expressions about time, in English or another language?

2. Imagine you are in the following situation:

- You make a plan to meet your friend for dinner at 6:30 p.m. You go to the meeting place at exactly 6:30 but she isn't there. How do you feel?

  _____

- It's 7:00, and she hasn't come. How do you feel now?

  _____

- It's 7:30, and she still has not arrived. How do you feel? _____

  What do you do? _____

Share your answers with a partner.

➤ AS YOU READ

Read "It's About Time" through quickly one time to get an idea of what the reading is about.

IT'S ABOUT TIME

1   Have you ever had trouble working with others because of their approach to time? Some people are prompt in completing their part of a project, while others are slow. Some people are on time for meetings, while others are late. Some people focus on getting the task done in time, while others spend time chatting and making 5 sure everyone is feeling comfortable. Why are we different in the ways we approach time?

2   Edward T. Hall, a famous sociologist,[1] found that there are cultural differences in perceiving time. He distinguished between two types of cultures—monochronic and polychronic. People of monochronic 10 cultures, such as northern Europeans and Anglo North Americans, tend to do one thing at a time. They value speed and punctuality. They are efficient and focused. They are controlled by their schedules. On the other hand, those in polychronic cultures, such as Latin and Arab countries, tend to do many things at once. They value flexibility 15 over punctuality and tend to change plans often and easily. They are controlled by human relationships more than their schedules. You may have heard of "Mexican time," "Brazilian time," or "Spanish time." This refers to the flexible approach to appointments and schedules in those countries: If you make a plan to meet your 20 Spanish friends for a drink at 9 p.m., they may come at 9:30 or 10:00 with no apology.

Monochronic Culture	*Polychronic Culture*
• Do one thing at a time	• Do several things at a time
• Tend to be punctual	• More flexible regarding schedule 25
• "Time is money"	• Business is a way of socializing
• Examples: USA, Germany, Japan	• Examples: France, Africa, Latin America

3   Of course, there are always exceptions to these cultural tendencies. That is to say, all Americans are not punctual, and all Spanish are not 30 relaxed about schedules. There are many individual differences. According to some psychologists, not only culture, but family and personality types also influence an individual's attitude to time. These psychologists divide people, not cultures, into monochronic

---

[1] *sociologist*: someone who studies the customs and beliefs of humans and society

and polychronic and say these are personality types found in every   35
culture. Monochronic people are organized, logical, and patient.
Polychronic people are creative, intuitive[2] and impulsive.[3]

4   Conflict happens when we try to apply a monochronic approach
to a situation that demands polychronic time, or vice-versa.[4] A
common example of this is if someone travels to a culture that   40
perceives time differently than in his or her own culture: English-
Canadian tourists (monochronic culture) may be frustrated by "slow"
restaurant service in Italy (polychronic culture). A polychronic
person may have trouble meeting all the deadlines at an American
university, since most American professors expect students to follow   45
the schedules strictly. Even in one's own culture, it may be difficult
for someone who is casual about appointments and deadlines to
work efficiently enough to satisfy a boss who values punctuality. And
someone who likes to follow a fixed work schedule will be upset by
a work-team or a boss who changes tasks or times without notice.   50

5   Perhaps most difficult is the fact that life requires both approaches to
time—some tasks, like taking out the garbage, are predictable and
can be approached in a monochronic way. However, a monochronic
approach doesn't apply to things like falling in love or resolving
an argument.   55

6   The next time you feel annoyed when someone keeps you waiting,
remember that people of different cultures, families, and personality
types may have different ideas of time. It is true that the late person
may be rude, lazy, or disrespectful. But if you are dealing with a
polychronic person, he or she is simply managing time differently   60
from the way you manage it. Likewise, if you are late for an appoint-
ment and your friend gets angry, remember that he or she may be
running on monochronic time. Respecting each other's different
attitudes to time may reduce conflict.

---

[2] *intuitive:* able to know something without being taught
[3] *impulsive:* acting suddenly without thought
[4] *vice-versa:* the other way around

➤VOCABULARY IN CONTEXT

Find each word or phrase in the paragraph indicated in brackets [ ]. From the context, guess the meaning. Then circle the best definition.

1. prompt [1]   **a.** without delay   **b.** late

2. perceiving [2]   **a.** seeing or noticing   **b.** forgetting

3. distinguished [2]   **a.** chose   **b.** made a difference

4. punctuality [2]   **a.** being late   **b.** being on time

5. flexibility [2]   **a.** the ability to change   **b.** the ability to be loyal
                            easily

6. tendencies [3]   **a.** habits which are   **b.** strange behaviors
                            usually followed

7. demands[4]   **a.** ignores   **b.** asks for

8. deadlines [4]   **a.** teachers   **b.** time limits

9. resolving [5]   **a.** finding a solution   **b.** creating something new
                            for

➤READING SKILL: Getting the Main Idea

Recognizing the *topic* (what the author is writing about) of a reading is the first step to understanding a reading. Identifying the *main idea* (what the author thinks about the topic) is the second step. When you know the main idea, you can recognize what is important and what you can skip over. Getting the main idea is essential for reading comprehension.

Example from Unit 3, Reading One:

Topic: Biodiversity

Main idea: Keeping biodiversity is important for human survival.

Often the author will state or imply the main idea near the end of the first paragraph and repeat it again in the last paragraph.

►READING SKILL PRACTICE: Getting the Main Idea

Part A

Skim each paragraph from Reading One. Ask yourself:

1. What is the topic? That is, what is the paragraph about? (1 to 4 words)

2. What is the main idea? That is, what does the author want me to understand about this topic? (A complete sentence)

For each paragraph, write the topic on the line. Then circle the best main idea (choose one). Paragraph 1 is done for you as an example.

Topic   **Main Idea**

Paragraph 1

_____Time_____   a. is perceived the same way by everyone.

                      ⓑ is approached differently by different people.

                      c. causes a lot of trouble at work.

Paragraph 2

_____   a. affects the way we perceive time.

                      b. is monochronic.

                      c. refers to a flexible approach to time.

Paragraph 3

_____   a. are not punctual.

                      b. cannot be changed.

                      c. also affect the perception of time.

Paragraph 4

_____   a. happens when someone travels to another culture.

                      b. happens between the two time systems.

                      c. happens in the American university system.

Paragraph 5

_____

a. is not predictable.

b. includes falling in love.

c. requires both approaches to time.

Paragraph 6

_____

a. may reduce conflict.

b. may be rude, lazy, or disrespectful.

c. creates conflict.

Part B

1. What is the topic of this whole reading?

_____ Culture and Time

_____ Being Punctual

_____ Monochronic Culture

2. Reread the first and last paragraphs, and underline the sentence(s) that summarize the main idea.

3. What is the main idea of this whole reading?

_____ People of polychronic cultures need to learn how to keep to deadlines and become more organized.

_____ Understanding the two cultural time systems, monochronic and polychronic, may be helpful in getting along with others.

_____ Everyone in the world should adopt the same approach to time since it is annoying when others are different.

➤ TAKING A CLOSER LOOK

Read the article again more carefully, looking for details. Decide if the following sentences are true (**T**) or false (**F**). Underline the sentence or phrase that supports your answer.

1. _____ Edward T. Hall found three different ways cultures perceive time.

2. _____ People of monochronic cultures tend to do many things at once.

3. _____ People of polychronic cultures are more casual about appointments.

4. _____ "Brazilian time" refers to the strict schedules in Brazil.

5. _____ A person with a polychronic personality may come from a monochronic culture.

6. _____ A polychronic person may be upset by a boss who changes tasks or times without notice.

7. _____ Both approaches to time occur in daily life.

8. _____ The author implies that falling in love cannot happen on schedule.

➤ COMMUNICATE: Interview

Students often complain about not having enough time. Most schools and universities approach time in a monochronic way. In American universities, for example, professors may fail students who are late. In other words, if you want to succeed at college, you might need to learn some monochronic time-management skills.

In this exercise you will talk to a partner about time-management habits. Use the following expressions in your conversation.

Sharing Experience	Asking for Clarification
In my experience . . .	Could you repeat that please?
I usually . . .	I'm sorry. I don't understand the question.
I often . . .	Did you say [ ]? How do you spell it?

Student A

- Ask your partner these questions about his or her time-management habits. Then describe your own habits. Finally, share the advice given in parentheses.

   1. How much time do you spend every week on (1) sleeping? (2) homework? (3) recreation?

      [Hint: Normal weekly sleep is 50–60 hours; normal homework time is 1 hour of homework for every hour in class; normal weekly time for recreation is about 10 hours.]

   2. How do you remember your assignment dates?

      [Hint: Write down long-term goals (e.g., essay or exam dates) on a calendar you can hang on the wall and see easily. Write short-term goals (weekly homework) in your daily schedule, which you should carry in your bag.]

- When Student B asks you questions, close your book so that you can pay attention to listening and speaking. If you don't understand, ask for clarification before answering.

Student B

- Close your book and listen to Student A's questions. If you don't understand, ask for clarification before answering.

- Then ask your partner these questions about his or her time-management habits. Describe your own habits. Finally, share the advice given in parentheses.

   1. How do you work on a big assignment? Do you try to do it in one night, or little by little?

      [Hint: Start the assignment on the day that it is assigned, then develop a plan for finishing it by dividing the task into 5 parts, with deadlines for yourself.]

   2. What time of day do you do your most difficult study?

      [Hint: Most of us have a high energy time and a low energy time each day. Find these times for yourself, and do the difficult work during your high energy time and the easy work during the lower time.]

➤ INTERACTIVE JOURNAL RESPONSE

Choose one of the following questions and write a response. Be prepared to give an oral summary of your written response in small groups.

1. Is your culture monochronic or polychronic? Are you monochronic or poly-chronic? Give examples to support your answer.

2. Have you ever had trouble when you tried to apply monochronic time to a polychronic situation, or vice-versa? Describe the experience, and explain how you could have avoided conflict by acting in a different way.

3. Use the Internet to search for advice on time management. List three pieces of information you learned from your Internet search.

READING TWO

➤ BEFORE YOU BEGIN

1. If you try to look up the word "timeshifting" in the dictionary, you won't find it! The author made it up. Check the meaning of "shift" in the dictionary, and then try to imagine what the author means by the term "timeshifting":

   I think the author might mean _____

   _____

   _____

2. Do you have "free time" in your daily life? How do you spend it? _____

   _____

   _____

➤ AS YOU READ

Now read "Timeshifting" through quickly one time, looking for the meaning of the term "timeshifting."

TIMESHIFTING: AN INTERVIEW WITH DR. STEPHAN RECHTSCHAFFEN

by Daniel Redwood

1   In his popular new book *Timeshifting*, Dr. Stephan Rechtschaffen discusses the habit of overwork existing in modern culture. He believes that many societies, including the United States, encourage us to live in "fast forward"—high speed—all the time. A high-

speed, high-stress lifestyle can cause high blood pressure and heart disease. It is healthier to learn how to "timeshift," to move smoothly from fast to medium to slow and back again. The following is an interview between Daniel Redwood and Stephan Rechtschaffen.

2   DR: Is staying busy always a positive thing?

3   SR: I don't think so. Too often we keep busy in order to avoid our real feelings. Painful feelings are difficult to face, and mostly we'd rather not feel them. So we substitute action for thinking and feeling. We get busy, speed up, turn on the television, do the chores, surf the Internet, go to the gym, anything to numb the painful feelings.

4   DR: What first led you to slow your pace?

5   SR: I want to make it clear that I'm not saying we need to do everything slowly. That's why I called my book *Timeshifting* rather than *Downshifting*. Timeshifting means constantly changing our rhythm, slowing or accelerating in order to feel in the present moment. In our society, we seem to lock into one particular speed—high speed.

6   DR: Is this strictly an American phenomenon?

7   SR: No. The Japanese even have a special word for it. Ten thousand people a year die from *karoshi* (death from overwork) in Japan. To officially qualify as a victim of *karoshi*, you have to have worked for at least 16 hours a day for seven straight days, or 24 hours straight just before dying. Yet when the Japanese government tried to shorten the work week from six days to five a few years ago, workers opposed the change.

8   DR: Why do people continue to work such long hours?

9   SR: When someone knows that staying longer at work will bring him or her increased income, there is a very strong incentive to stay longer and longer. A conflict develops. The person asks, "Do I leave work now and spend some time with my kids before they go to bed, maybe read them a story, or do I keep on going with this project here at work?" More and more people are choosing to stay at work. The problem is, we lose sight of our original goals. The goal is not to make money. The goal is to have the time and enjoyment that money can provide. But if we just stay at work, earning more and more money, we don't take the time to enjoy life, to read that story to the child. Then what is the point of it all?

10   DR: How about the common ways we spend our free time?

11   SR: It's hard for people to really slow down even in their free time. Speed, action, and busyness are addictive.[1] The Japanese hobby of *pachinko*, the pinball gambling game, is an effective way to enter a sort of hypnotic trance,[2] to keep yourself from feeling. You might think you are relaxing, but you are really just numbing yourself. Too much of this can be stressful for the mind and body.

12   DR: Is there an American equivalent?

13   SR: Television. Research shows that approximately 40 percent of the average American's free time goes straight into television. And again, it serves to remove us from feeling, from the direct experience of our own lives.

14   DR: What are some good ways to deeply relax, to reconnect to our lives?

15   SR: There are many ways to do it. Meditation, listening to music, taking a walk in nature. Sometimes the best thing is to just sit still in one place for an hour.

---

[1] *addictive:* difficult to stop (as in a habit like smoking)
[2] *hypnotic trance:* a sleep-like state

➤ VOCABULARY IN CONTEXT

Find each word or phrase in the paragraph indicated in brackets [ ]. From the context, guess the meaning. Then circle the best definition.

1. substitute [3]   a. keep   b. replace

2. numb [3]   a. take away the power to feel   b. give the power to feel

3. accelerating [5]   a. speeding up   b. slowing down

4. phenomenon [6]   a. workplace   b. event or occurrence

5. opposed [7]   a. supported   b. spoke against

6. incentive [9]   a. punishment   b. reward, encouragement

7. equivalent [12]   a. something similar   b. something different

➤ READING SKILL PRACTICE: Getting the Main Idea

Part A

For each paragraph, write the topic on the line. Then circle the best main idea.

Paragraph 1

Topic

_____

Main Idea

a. is a popular new book.

b. is important to learn because living at high speed is unhealthy.

c. means changing one's pace.

Paragraph 3

_____

a. helps people avoid their real feelings.

b. is always a positive thing.

c. is difficult to stop.

Paragraph 5

_____

     a. means slowing down.

     b. means changing our rhythm.

     c. is the same as Downshifting.

Part B

The topic is given for the following paragraphs. Write the main idea in a complete sentence.

Topic   **Main Idea**

Paragraph 7

Overwork in Japan   _____

Paragraph 9

Overwork   _____

Paragraph 11

Free Time   _____

Part C

Read each paragraph and write the topic (1 to 3 words) and the main idea (a complete sentence).

Topic   **Main Idea**

Paragraph 13

_____   _____

Paragraph 15

_____   _____

Part D

What is the topic of this whole interview?

_____ timeshifting   _____ overwork   _____ slowing down

Part E

1. Reread the first and last paragraphs, and underline the sentences that summarize the main idea of the whole interview.

2. What is the main idea of this whole interview?

    _____ It is an interview with a doctor who explains how and why to change our daily pace of living by "timeshifting."

    _____ It is an article about the science fiction idea of timeshifting, moving backwards and forwards in time.

    _____ It is an interview with a doctor who is worried that people in modern society are becoming lazy and wasting time by "timeshifting."

►TAKING A CLOSER LOOK

Read the article again more carefully, looking for details. Decide if the following sentences are true (T) or false (F). Highlight the sentence or phrase which supports your answer.

1. _____ A high-speed life can cause heart disease.

2. _____ Dr. Rechtschaffen thinks we should slow our pace.

3. _____ He thinks we get busy in order to feel our emotions more deeply.

4. _____ Working at high speed is not only an American phenomenon.

5. _____ When the Japanese government tried to shorten the work week to five days, the workers said no.

6. _____ The Japanese game of baseball is an effective way to enter a hypnotic trance.

7. _____ Twenty percent of Americans' free time is spent watching television.

8. _____ Watching television is a good way to relax.

9. _____ Dr. Rechtschaffen thinks that the goal of life is to make money.

► COMMUNICATE: Interview

Consider the following questions about your own lifestyle. Then interview your partner. Change roles so that both of you have a chance to be the interviewer. Be sure not to read your partner's paper.

	You	Your partner
1. How many hours a day do you work or study?	_____	_____
How many hours a day do you relax?	_____	_____

	You	Your partner
2. How do you spend your free time.	_____	_____
Do you "speed up" or "slow down?"	_____	_____

Ways to Speed Up	Ways to Slow Down
turn on the TV	practice meditation
do the chores	listen to music
surf the Internet	take a walk in nature
go to the gym	sit still

	You	Your partner
3. Do you prefer speeding up or slowing down?	_____	_____
Do you think your life is balanced enough?	_____	_____
Do you think you need to "timeshift"?	_____	_____

Use the following expressions in your interview.

Asking for clarification or repetition	Active Listening
Do you mind if I ask you a few questions about [your lifestyle] ?	I see.
	Oh?
Can you give me an example?	Mmm.
Can you explain that?	Really!
Could you repeat that please?	Yes.
Do you mean ...?	

➤ INTERACTIVE JOURNAL RESPONSE

Choose one of the following questions and write a response. Be prepared to give an oral summary of your written response in small groups.

1. Is there any need for "timeshifting" in your culture? How about in your own life?

2. Do you personally know anyone who "timeshifts"? If so, describe that person's lifestyle.

GREEN BUSINESS

ALUMINIUM
DRINKS CAN
RECYCLING POINT

A green business is environmentally responsible. A green business limits its pollution and uses renewable resources in the manufacture of its products. The rule of a green business is to "reduce

READING ONE

➤ BEFORE YOU BEGIN

1. What "green" products have you noticed while shopping? Would you buy any of them? Why or why not?

2. Read the title of Reading One. Look up the word "chic" in your dictionary if you are not sure of its meaning. What do you think "Rainforest Chic" might mean? Give some examples of what "Rainforest Chic" might include.

3. Skim the first two paragraphs of the reading. Did you include some of the same examples in your answer to question 2?

4. From the information you have gathered, what do you think this reading will be about?

➤ AS YOU READ

Read " 'Rainforest Chic': Green Economics in the Amazon" through quickly to get the main idea.

'RAINFOREST CHIC': GREEN ECONOMICS IN THE AMAZON
by William R. Long (from *The Los Angeles Times*)

1   Rio De Janeiro—From Brazil's Amazon forest to the shelves of the American supermarket is a long way, but a growing variety of rainforest "chic" is making the journey. New soaps, shampoos, and lotions are introducing American consumers to Amazonian copaiba oil, a pale yellow oil tapped from the copaiba tree by forest people. Cookies [5] and candies are being made in the United States containing Brazil nuts harvested in the Amazon. Cultural Survival, a nonprofit corporation[1] based in Cambridge, Massachusetts, established this green business. The business is based on the concept that tropical forests can be preserved by helping forest people make a living without cutting [10] them down. And as consumers learn about the importance of saving the rainforest, Cultural Survival has become more popular.

2   For the past several years, Cultural Survival has been buying nuts, forest fruits, and other rainforest commodities, mostly from the

---

[1] *nonprofit corporation:* a company that does not have making money as its primary aim

Brazilian Amazon region, and reselling them to American manu- 15
facturers. Cultural Survival's list of consumer products containing
tropical commodities rose from 19 to about 100 in just one year.
New ones being developed include fruit drinks, dried fruits, nut
mixes, lip balm, and bath beads.

3   Market growth[2] has been so fast that Cultural Survival has been 20
able to buy only a small percentage of its forest supplies directly from
forest people. To help organize forest communities and develop its
supply network, Cultural Survival set up a branch office in Brazil.
"A lot of communities don't have products available in the quantity
and quality needed to participate," said Diana Propper de Callejon, 25
the manager in Brazil. "We hope to help them develop so they can
eventually supply us with all our forest commodities."

4   So far, Brazil nuts gathered in the Amazonian state of Acre and
copaiba oil collected in the neighboring state of Rondonia are the
only important supplies coming directly from forest people. 30
Commercial suppliers[3] provide the rest of what Cultural Survival
needs. But income from commercially supplied commodities is used
for tropical forest conservation projects and to help forest communities. Under contracts with its customers, Cultural Survival receives
varying shares of profits from products made with forest commodities. 35
For example, Rainforest Essentials Co. of Santa Monica returns 40
percent of the profits from its shampoo, soap, and hair conditioner—
all containing copaiba. Lyn Nelson, president of Rainforest Essentials
Co., said in a telephone interview that sales of the products have
boomed since marketing began. 40

5   "People really respond to this idea," she said. "When they buy,
they feel like they are making a contribution, which they are."
And copaiba is "an amazing oil," she said. "It's just so moisturizing and
nourishing." Because of consumer demand, Rainforest Essentials
Co. is planning to add more products with rainforest ingredients. 45

6   Ben Cohen, an East Coast entrepreneur[4] who makes Rainforest
Crunch candy with Brazil nuts from Cultural Survival, said sales
exceeded $2 million in the first full year of its marketing. Half of

---

[2] *market growth:* the increase in consumer demand for a product
[3] *commercial suppliers:* people or companies who produce a product in big enough
   quantities to make a profit.
[4] *entrepreneur:* a person developing a new business at the risk of failure

the candy production is used in ice cream made by another of
Cohen's companies, Ben & Jerry's. "The product took off[5] better
than we ever expected it would," Cohen said by telephone from
Vermont, where the companies are based. "I think this is a combination of its tasting really good and people wanting to do what
they can to help with the rainforest situation. We're creating bigger
and bigger demand for Brazil nuts and therefore their value is
increasing." That gives Brazilians more reason to protect forests
where the nuts grow.

7   Currently, Cultural Survival buys about a quarter of its commodities directly from producers in the rainforest and the rest
from commercial suppliers. In addition to Amazon products, the
group imports honey and beeswax from Zambia and Tanzania,
banana chips from the Philippines, cashew nuts from Honduras
and macadamia nuts from Costa Rica. Manufacturers pay a 5 percent
"environmental tax" for the commodities and agree to share some
profits for Cultural Survival rainforest projects. Cultural Survival
hopes to set up a loan fund to help tropical producers using the
money from the environmental tax they collect and the profits
shares they take in.

8   Jason Clay, Cultural Survival's project director, is researching
how best to make this green business work. His latest idea is to
use dirigibles[6] to airlift forest products, such as Brazil nuts and
copaiba oil, out of remote Amazon areas instead of building roads
into the forest. His ultimate goal is to make preservation of rainforests so profitable that cutting them down would be impractical.
"I think rainforests are going to have to generate income or they're
going to be lost," he said.

---

[5] *took off:* became popular
[6] *dirigibles:* air ships with a steering device

► GETTING THE MAIN IDEA

Check the statement you think best expresses the main idea of this reading.
Then compare your answer with your classmates.

1. _____ Cultural Survival is helping to save the rainforest.

2. _____ Money can be made from rainforest products.

3. _____ The number of rainforest products is increasing in America.

➤ VOCABULARY IN CONTEXT

Find each word or phrase in the paragraph indicated in brackets [ ]. From the context, guess the meaning. Then circle the best definition.

1. consumers [1]   **a.** people who buy   **b.** people who sell

2. preserved [1]   **a.** selected   **b.** protected

3. commodities [2]   **a.** activities   **b.** products for sale

4. income [4]   **a.** money earned   **b.** extra help

5. boomed [4]   **a.** increased   **b.** decreased

6. contribution [5]   **a.** something given   **b.** something destroyed

7. remote [8]   **a.** opposite   **b.** faraway

8. ultimate [8]   **a.** final   **b.** unusual

➤ TAKING A CLOSER LOOK

Read " 'Rainforest Chic': Green Economics in the Amazon" again. Decide if the following sentences are true (**T**) or false (**F**). Underline the sentence or phrase that supports your answer.

1. _____ The goal of Cultural Survival is to help forest people cut down their trees.

2. _____ So far, forest people have enough forest products to supply Cultural Survival.

3. _____ Cultural Survival is introducing new forest products to its consumers.

4. _____ Consumers are not really interested in buying rainforest products.

5. _____ Some of the profits from sales of rainforest products are used to help forest communities.

6. _____ Ben and Jerry's ice cream was not really popular in the beginning.

7. _____ Cultural Survival only uses forest products from the Amazon.

8. _____ Jason Clay thinks rainforests cannot be saved unless they make money.

➤ READING SKILL: Scanning for Details

As a student, you may be asked to scan for details—dates, numbers, names, vocabulary—and other information. One of the best ways to find details is to scan—to move your eyes quickly down the page in search of the information you are looking for. Use the following strategies when scanning for details:

- Use key words from the question or statement to help you find details. For example, if the statement reads, " The profits from Rainforest Crunch are . . . ", use the key words "profits" and "Rainforest Crunch" as you scan for the information you need.

- If you are looking for a date, then look for numbers, commas, and names of months and days of the week.

- If you are looking for a name, then look for capital letters and abbreviations (Co., Ltd., and so forth).

- If you are looking for details such as definitions, terms, concepts, or comments, then look for punctuation: words inside quotations (" "), commas (,), dashes (—), and words in parentheses ( ). Words in *italics*, and underlined words also signal details.

➤ READING SKILL PRACTICE: Scanning for Details

Use the clues above for scanning to complete the following sentences based on the information from Reading One. Then compare your answers with your classmates.

1. Copaiba oil is a pale yellow oil tapped by _____.

   a. American consumers

   b. forest people

   c. nonprofit corporations

2. _____ is a nonprofit corporation trying to preserve the Amazon rainforest by doing business directly with the forest people.

   a. Ben & Jerry's

   b. Cultural Survival

   c. Rainforest Crunch

3. The list of Cultural Survival's products using tropical commodities increased from _____ in just one year.

   a. $1 to $2 million

   b. 19 to 100

   c. 17 to 40

4. The manager of Cultural Survival's branch office in Brazil is _____.

   a. Ben Cohen

   b. Diana Propper de Callejon

   c. Lyn Nelson

5. Brazil nuts are gathered in the state of _____.

   a. Rondonia

   b. Massachusetts

   c. Acre

6. The company that makes ice cream is called _____.

   a. Rainforest Crunch

   b. Ben & Jerry's

   c. Cultural Survival

7. Manufacturers pay Cultural Survival a 5 percent _____.

   a. profits share

   b. environmental tax

   c. market growth

8. Jason Clay wants to use _____ to transport forest products out of the rainforest.

   a. roads

   b. dirigibles

   c. railroads

➤**COMMUNICATE: Company Evaluation**

While some companies are truly interested in exploring ways to protect the environment, others claim to be "green" but do nothing to make their product environmentally friendly. How can a consumer be sure that when they buy they are making a contribution towards protecting the environment? The following guide is used as one way to evaluate how "green" a company really is.

A Green Consumer's Guide

1. Products are made from recycled material or renewable resources taken in a way that does not damage the environment.

2. Products are long-lasting and reusable. They can be recycled or are truly biodegradable.

3. Products use minimal packaging.

4. Product information on manufacturing, such as location, labor practices, and animal testing is stated clearly, and the manufacturer's web site or contact address is supplied.

Look at the product information from the Body Shop, a business that is known to operate under green business policies.

The Body Shop is an international specialty retailer that develops, manufactures and sells innovative hair, skin, and color cosmetic products. Founder Anita Roddick opened her first shop in Brighton, England in 1976. There are now more than 2,000 shops worldwide.

From our best-selling Peppermint Foot Lotion to our innovative Brazil Nut Conditioner; our special Animals in Danger line for children to our Activist Aftershave Spray for men, our products provide high quality and value for people who care about themselves and their world.

The business practices of the Body Shop are defined by our core values: caring for the environment through renewable and sustainable resources; managing waste, reducing pollution, and improving energy efficiency in our operations; raising awareness through training and education; and a commitment to full disclosure of our environmental assets.

To learn more about profits with principles, contact:
The Body Shop
5036 One World Way
Wake Forest, NC 27587

Work in a small group. Choose a group member to take notes as you evaluate.

1. Read the product information.

2. Evaluate the company by comparing what the product information says with the guidelines from "A Green Consumer's Guide." From the information you have gathered, do you think this company operates a green business? Why or why not?

3. Share your evaluation with other groups in the class.

Use the following expressions to help you express your ideas as you evaluate.

> **Stating your opinions**
>
> I think the Body Shop is . . . because it follows number(s) ... from the Green Consumer's Guide.
>
> In my opinion the Body Shop is not a green business because ...
>
> I definitely agree with you.
>
> I disagree with what you say. I think ...

➤ INTERACTIVE JOURNAL RESPONSE

Choose one of the following questions and write a response. Be prepared to give an oral summary of your written response in small groups.

1. Ben Cohen of Ben & Jerry's ice cream believes the company's ice cream is popular in the United States because of "a combination of its tasting really good and people wanting to do what they can to help with the rainforest situation." Do you think people in your country would buy this product for the same reasons? Why or why not?

2. Jason Clay, marketing director of Cultural Survival, says his ultimate goal is to make preservation of rainforests so profitable that cutting them down would be impractical. He believes that "rainforests are going to have to generate income or they're going to be lost." Do you agree with him? Why or why not?

3. Based on Reading One, what difficulties might Cultural Survival and similar companies face in trying to operate under green policies?

READING TWO

➤ BEFORE YOU BEGIN

1. Do you think your purchasing habits (the things you choose to buy) have an effect on other people's lives or the environment? Why or why not?

2. Survey the following reading to predict the contents. Read the title. Use the scanning skills you learned in Reading One to find the definition of the word "Seikatsu." Finally, read the section headings.

3. From the information you have gathered, what do you think this reading will be about?

> ►AS YOU READ

Read through "Seikatsu Club: Japanese Housewives Organize" quickly to get the main idea.

SEIKATSU CLUB: JAPANESE HOUSEWIVES ORGANIZE

by Shigeki Maruyama, *Green Business: Hope or Hoax?*

1   Cooperatives have frequently been used by people who want to move beyond conventional business forms, even if only to buy together, or, in a more developed form, to own, manage, and run their own [5] enterprises. In Japan, a group of housewives has taken the cooperative model several strides forward to involve an environmental aspect, a philosophy that embraces all of life. Run by a board of directors that [10] comprises 80 percent women, the *Seikatsu* (activities of daily life) *Club* has been putting a broad range of progressive principles into practice successfully for many years.

[15]

Principles of the Seikatsu Club

2   What started as a strategy to save money gradually developed over the next 20 years into a philosophy of life. In addition to cost-effective[1] collective purchases, the club is committed to a host of social concerns, including: (1) the environment; (2) the empowerment of women; [20] (3) workers' conditions.

3   The Seikatsu Club believes that their business should be run by their own investments.[2] This is part of the club's vision to reduce the division between producer, consumer, and investor. When members join the co-op, they make an initial investment of 1,000 yen ($8.00). [25] This, supplemented by monthly contributions of 1,000 yen, brings

---

[1] *cost-effective:* giving value for money
[2] *investments:* money put into starting or developing a business

the average investment to roughly 47,000 yen (about \$435.00) per person, which is returned whenever a member leaves the co-op. This investment strategy has been highly successful. The primary function of the club is not to sell but to buy. Unlike most Japanese co-ops, which distribute goods through their stores, the club delivers goods to its members. Individual members have no real buying power in the Club. A "han," composed of 6 to 13 families, is the basic unit for making a purchase. Everything is bought in bulk; for example, a minimum of 15 cartons of milk or seven kilograms of eggs. These are distributed to one location where each family picks up their purchases.

Respecting the Environment

4   The club refuses to handle products if they are detrimental to the health of the members or the environment. Synthetic[3] detergents, artificial seasoning, and clothing treated with chemicals are all off limits, even if members make demands for them. The club gets safer produce by cooperating with local farmers. In return for asking them to use organic[4] fertilizer and fewer chemicals, members buy a contracted amount of produce and agree to overlook any physical imperfections. Members also assist farmers with the harvest when their labor is necessary. The Seikatsu Club stands by the belief that housewives can begin to create a society that is harmonious with nature by "taking action from the home." And through their purchases and consumption, they are attempting to change the way that Japanese agriculture and fisheries are operated.

5   When the club cannot find products that meet the quality, ecological, or social standards, they will consider starting their own businesses. This can be illustrated by the two organic milk production facilities they currently run with local dairy farmers. Buying directly from producers does more than merely eliminate the added distribution cost of the middleman.[5] It enhances cooperation and awareness by keeping consumers in touch with[6] the production process.

---

[3] *synthetic:* artificial

[4] *organic:* made from natural matter

[5] *middleman:* person who take goods from the producer and distributes them to stores

[6] *in touch with:* knowing about

From Soap to City Council

6   Started in 1974, the club's soap movement offers a fine example of environmental awareness and how "the kitchen" can provide an effective starting point for a political movement. After noticing cracked skin on their own hands and skin irritation on their babies, housewives began to question synthetic soaps. Their protests succeeded in getting synthetic detergents off the shelves of their co-op shops, and as a result, *shirauo*, a whitefish sensitive to pollution, began to return to the town river.

7   Because of larger community environmental concerns, the club members then went to their local government, asking for a law to be passed that would eliminate the use of synthetic detergents in their area. Although the law was not passed, they received recognition and through their campaigning on the slogan "Political Reform from the Kitchen," the club succeeded in getting 33 members elected to the local government. This success has attracted the attention of women all over the country. The club has given women, historically isolated in the home, a vehicle for political involvement.

8   The Seikatsu Club started life as a way of saving money. Today, concerns include environmental quality, women's working conditions, and public health. The Seikatsu Club is just one example of a network of people who seek to make changes for a better future.

➤ GETTING THE MAIN IDEA

Check the statement you think best expresses the main idea of this reading. Then compare your answer with your classmates.

1. _____ The Seikatsu Club is a strong cooperative in Japan.

2. _____ Japanese women are a strong force in Japanese society these days.

3. _____ The Seikatsu Club is committed to making life in Japan better.

►VOCABULARY IN CONTEXT

The following words can be found in the reading passage. Scan each paragraph indicated in brackets [ ] to find the word. Read the sentence or paragraph the word is found in to guess its meaning from context. Then use the words to complete the sentences below.

embraces [1]	strategy [2]	distributed [3]	bulk [3]
detrimental [4]	imperfection [4]	harmonious [4]	
eliminate [5]	sensitive [6]	network [8]	

1. The class worked together in a _____ way. Everyone got along so well.

2. They bought all their food in _____ because they had such a large family.

3. I noticed the _____ on the shirt right away. I could see that the left side of the shirt was longer than the right side.

4. His eyes were so _____ he had to wear sunglasses even when it was cloudy.

5. The paper boy _____ newspapers to everyone in the office.

6. The question was unclear so the teachers decided to _____ it from the test.

7. There was a _____ of small streets leading from the water-front to the center of town.

8. What _____ should I use to teach a young child to read?

9. An increase in taxes by the government could be _____ to the future of the company.

10. She _____ many of the new ideas her company members suggest to her.

➤ TAKING A CLOSER LOOK

Read "Seikatsu Club: Japanese Housewives Organize" again, this time focusing on details. Decide if the following sentences are true (**T**) or false (**F**). Underline the sentence or phrase that supports your answer.

1. _____ The Seikatsu Club was first started to give women more power in the home.

2. _____ All club members must pay a monthly fee.

3. _____ Club members buy their food and goods at the local Seikatsu Club store.

4. _____ Buying large quantities is not possible through the Seikatsu Club.

5. _____ The Seikatsu Club sells only natural products.

6. _____ The club members believe it is important to take action from the home.

7. _____ The soap movement caused a town river to become polluted.

8. _____ Through the action of the Seikatsu Club, synthetic detergents were banned by the government.

➤ READING SKILL: Scanning for Details

As a student you may be required to read long, densely written readings from a textbook. Your reading assignment, however, may have a special purpose, for example, to find a definition, to look for a concept, or to pick out other specific information. To find this information it is absolutely essential to scan. The following clues will help you with these types of reading assignments.

- First, make sure you know what you are looking for. What is the teacher asking you to identify? What information do you have to find in the reading?

- Look for subtitles and numbered or specially marked sections to locate information.

- If you are looking for specific principles or a list of points, scan the page for words or phrases set off by numbers or letters, (1, 2; a, b), by bullets (•), or special punctuation such as a comma (,), semicolon (;) or colon (:).

- When looking for definitions, scan the page for words in *italics*, words in quotations (" "), information in parentheses ( ) or a dash —— after a word.

➤ **READING SKILL PRACTICE: Scanning for Details**

Fill in the answers to the following questions using the clues for scanning.

1. Locate the subtitles in this reading and write them below.

   _____ _____ _____

2. What are the three social concerns of the Seikatsu Club?

   (1) _____ (2) _____ (3) _____

3. Define the word "han" used in this reading.

   _____

4. What examples are used for buying in bulk?

   _____ _____

5. Under what subtitle would you look for information concerning the club's environmental concerns?

   _____

6. In what year did the club's soap movement start? _____

7. What is the name of the whitefish that has been saved because of the Seikatsu Club? _____

8. What other issues are the Seikatsu Club members interested in these days?

   _____ _____ _____

COMMUNICATE: Class Survey

What do your classmates look for when choosing a product?

1. Think of three or four products your classmates might buy on a regular basis (they could be related to food, entertainment, cosmetics, bath products, and so forth). Write them in the chart that follows.

2. Survey your classmates by placing an X in the space to indicate the responses of your classmates. Be sure to add any interesting comments they have.

Product	Reasons for Choice					Comments
	Quality	Price	Brand name	Packaging	Environmentally friendly	
shampoo			X		X	It smells nice.

Use the following expressions when conducting your survey.

Opening Remarks	
I'd like to ask you some questions about your purchasing habits. Would you mind answering my questions?	
Conducting the Survey	
Which factor do you consider most important when buying _____? Is it the price, the brand name ...?	
Asking for more Ideas	**Closing Remarks**
Do you have anything else to add? Do you have any other comments?	Thank you for your time. Thanks for your comments.

3. Go through your chart to find out the most common reason your class-mates gave for choosing each product.

4. Finally, share and discuss your survey results with the rest of the class.

►INTERACTIVE JOURNAL RESPONSE

Choose one of the following questions and write a response. Be prepared to give an oral summary of your written response in small groups.

1. The Seikatsu Club bases its operations on interdependent relationships. What are some examples to illustrate this interdependence? Scan paragraphs 4, 5, and 6 to find some examples.

2. Do you think the Seikatsu Club would be popular in your country? Why or why not?

3. What is your view of green business? Do you think green business can help improve the environment, or is it just a way to attract consumers?

BEAUTY

E ach person has his or her own idea about what is "beautiful."
But perhaps even stronger than our individual preferences is our
cultural view. Each culture has its stereotype of "beautiful women"
and "handsome men," and these stereotypes change over time

READING ONE

➤ BEFORE YOU BEGIN

1. What do you associate with the word "beauty?" Make a list of five things that come to mind: _____

   _____

   _____

2. In your culture, who spends more time and money on their appearance, men or women? Why?

3. Describe a typically handsome American man.

➤ AS YOU READ

Read "The New Man" through quickly one time, looking for the main idea.

THE NEW MAN
by Stephen Henderson (excerpted from *The New York Times*)

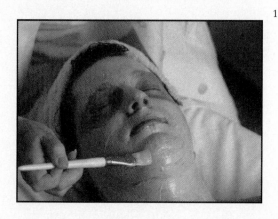

1   Not long ago, Elise Berenzweig's mother telephoned to say she'd spotted Elise's husband, Evan, dallying[1] on a weekday afternoon at a suburban New Jersey nail salon. Elise took this news in stride[2], guessing that Evan had added manicures to what she terms his "going at it full force" beauty regimen[3].

2   "I am proud that my husband wants to look so good," Mrs. Berenzweig said. "Evan is very aesthetic[4]. It's important to him."

3   Just how important, he doesn't hesitate to say. "I'm obsessed[5] about

---

[1] *dallying:* taking a long time; delaying
[2] *took this news in stride:* was not surprised to hear the news
[3] *regimen:* program
[4] *aesthetic:* artistic, appreciating beauty
[5] *obsessed:* very concerned; thinking about only one thing

keeping my pants size," said Mr. Berenzweig, 42. He maintains a year-round tan (bolstered[6] in wintertime, he concedes[7], with a bronzing cream) and schedules frequent "industrial strength" teeth cleanings, massages and pedicures. Some "eye work" may be in his future.

4   "I am vain, but I'm not conceited[8]," Mr. Berenzweig explained. "besides, women friends of mine implore their husbands to be more like me."

5   Attention please, beer-gut[9] Gus, hairy Harry, and turkey-neck Tom. Wake up and smell the skin conditioner before women start imploring you to join men across America who are paying more attention to, and more money for, their personal appearance. At all ages and incomes, a steadily growing number of men are tightening their muscles, filing their fingernails, having their smiles whitened and eyes "undrooped"—or worrying that they should.

6   "It's O.K. for a man to improve himself in ways that were at one time considered artificial or, even worse, feminine," said Dr. Larry Rosenthal, a cosmetic dentist on the Upper East Side, who offers a one-day "smile lift" for $15,000.

7   An increase in male vanity is occurring now for a variety of reasons, experts say. Some cite the baby boom generation's[10] fear of aging, coupled with younger men's acceptance that they will be judged by their appearance—a conviction reinforced by advertisements. Others make the point that today's self-reliant women, with incomes of their own, have forced men to shape up because career women can afford to be alone rather than live with a Neanderthal.[11]

8   "The perception among men that they are going to be judged, at least initially, by their appearance is quite new," said Dr. James Perlotto, a family physician in New Haven, who is also a professor of medicine at Yale Medical School. "In the baby boomer generation, among men in their 30's, 40s, 50's, it often creates a unique fear of aging. Guys in their teens and 20's, on the other hand, put more value on the surface of things, how they dress, wear their hair.

---

[6] *bolstered:* supported, made stronger

[7] *concedes:* admits

[8] *conceited:* having too high an opinion of one's own beauty

[9] *beer-gut:* big stomach caused by drinking too much beer

[10] *baby boom generation:* people born between the years of 1950 and 1965; also known in America as the "me" generation

[11] *Neanderthal:* primitive human

9   The shift in thinking has produced insecurities in some men about their appearance, suggesting that men are now internalizing the same social message that women have suffered under for decades—that their worth is based on their looks.   50

10   The five top cosmetic procedures for men, starting with the most popular, are hair transplantation, nose reshaping, liposuction,[12] chemical peels, and collagen injections. . . With a growing group of male clients, Dr. Alan Matarasso has even equipped his office on Park Avenue and 84th Street with a separate entrance for men to   55 ensure their privacy. . . . "What we do in plastic surgery you can't achieve alone. Even if you go to the gym, you can't take the bump out of your nose, get rid of a turkey neck or that droop in your eyelid."

11   Far from shy about anything related to personal beautification, Evan Berenzweig is now busily passing along a lifetime of trade   60 secrets to his three growing sons. "When Evan was young, he thought he had blackheads on his nose," his wife said. Determined to spare their eldest son, Addison, a similar fate, "Evan's already prepping him," she said, adding, "He bought Addison cleansing pads and showed him how to use them. Sometimes they go together   65 to get facials." How old is Addison? "He's 12," Mrs. Berenzweig said, with a mother's pride, "And he's very good looking."

---

[12] *liposuction:* a surgical operation to remove fat from the human body

►GETTING THE MAIN IDEA

Read the following sentences. Which one do you think expresses the author's main idea?

1. _____ In recent years, American men are more interested in improving their health.

2. _____ In recent years, American men are more interested in looking good.

3. _____ American women are forcing men to take better care of their appearance.

➤ **VOCABULARY IN CONTEXT**

Find each word in the paragraph indicated in brackets [ ]. Determine the meaning of the word from the sentences. Circle the best definition.

1. spotted [1]   a. seen   b. lost

2. implore [4]   a. ignore   b. ask strongly

3. vain [4]   a. caring too much   b. caring too much about
                             about one's family   one's appearance
                             members

4. coupled with [7]   a. joined together   b. separated from

5. reinforced [7]   a. made weaker   b. made stronger

6. self reliant [7]   a. independent   b. weak

7. shift [9]   a. stop   b. change

8. internalizing [9]   a. accepting, taking   b. rejecting, putting outside
                             inside

9. hair   a. moving hair from   b. changing an old-fashioned
   transplantation [10]   one place to another   hair style to a new one
                             on the body

10. equipped [10]   a. taken away what is   b. supplied what is needed
                             not necessary

➤ **READING SKILL: Paraphrasing**

To paraphrase means to put the information of a sentence into your own words. As you read a difficult sentence, replace difficult words and phrases with simple ones, while keeping the same meaning. This is a learning strategy which will help you think in English (rather than translate into your native language) when you are faced with difficult reading.

There are two steps to paraphrasing: 1) changing the difficult vocabulary to simple vocabulary, and 2) changing the grammar by using your own English. Look at the following example of paraphrasing from the third paragraph of "The New Man":

Original phrasing:

He maintains a year-round tan (bolstered in wintertime, he concedes, with a bronzing cream) . . . [paragraph 3]

Paraphrase (same meaning; easier words and grammar):

He admits that he keeps tanned year-round by using a bronzing cream in wintertime to support the tan.

►READING SKILL PRACTICE: Paraphrasing by Replacing Difficult Words

The first step in paraphrasing is to change the difficult vocabulary to simple vocabulary. You may need to use your dictionary to find suitable words.

Look at the example again:

Original: He <u>maintains</u> a year-round tan (<u>bolstered</u> in wintertime, he <u>concedes</u>, with a bronzing cream.)

maintains → keeps

bolstered → supported

concedes → admits

By substituting the difficult words, you can begin the first step of paraphrasing:

Paraphrase: He keeps a year-round tan (supported in wintertime, he admits, with a bronzing cream.)

Use your dictionary to find easy words or phrases to replace the underlined difficult words or idioms.

1. *Original:* Women friends of mine <u>implore</u> their husbands to be more like me [paragraph 4]

   Paraphrase: _____

   _____

2. *Original:* An increase in male <u>vanity</u> is <u>occurring</u> now for a variety of reasons. [paragraph 7]

Paraphrase: _____

_____

_____

3. *Original:* The <u>shift</u> in thinking has produced <u>insecurities</u> in some men about their appearance, suggesting that men are now <u>internalizing</u> the same social message that women have suffered under for decades. [paragraph 9]

Paraphrase: _____

_____

4. *Original:* Dr. Matarasso has even <u>equipped</u> his office on Park Avenue with a separate entrance for men to <u>ensure</u> their privacy. [paragraph 10]

Paraphrase: _____

_____

➤TAKING A CLOSER LOOK

Read the article again more carefully, this time focusing on details. Decide if the following sentences are true (**T**) or false (**F**). Underline the sentence or phrase that supports your answer.

1. _____ Evan's wife was embarrassed that Evan was seen having a manicure.

2. _____ Evan thinks enjoying delicious food is more important than staying slim.

3. _____ It is only young men who are paying more attention to their appearance.

4. _____ Advertising may be influencing men to believe they will be judged by their appearance.

5. _____ One possible reason for the increase in male vanity is that today's women are self-reliant.

6. _____ Men refuse to admit that their worth is based on their looks.

7. _____ Hair transplantation is the most popular cosmetic procedure for men.

8. _____ Evan's wife is busy teaching beauty secrets to their three sons.

► COMMUNICATE: Examining Beliefs

Examine your beliefs by filling out the following values chart.

1. First, fill out the chart by yourself. Check the column that matches your opinion, for men and for women.

2. Compare your ideas with a partner. This is a speaking and listening activity, so don't look at your partner's paper. Ask and answer questions, sharing your opinions.

How do you feel about men and women doing the following activities for their beauty?

	Important to do		OK to do		Not OK to do	
	Men	Women	Men	Women	Men	Women
1. Manicure						
2. Facial						
3. Diet						
4. Tanning						
5. Whitening teeth						
6. Face lift						
7. Muscle building						
8. Hair transplantation						
9. Nose reshape						
10. Liposuction						
11. Makeup						
12. Hair dye						

Use the following expressions in your discussion.

Asking for an opinion	Stating your personal belief	Summarizing a judgment
How do you feel about [men/women having a manicure]?	As far as I'm concerned . . .	It seems that you/I have [conservative/typical/liberal] beliefs about [beauty and gender roles].
	I feel that . . .	
What do you think about . . . ?	Personally, I believe . . .	
Which columns did you check for number 1?		

➤ INTERACTIVE JOURNAL RESPONSE

Choose one of the following questions and write a response. Be prepared to give an oral summary of your written response in small groups.

1. Were you surprised by this reading? Why or why not?

2. Do you think it is important to spend time and money on looking good? Why or why not?

3. Describe the stereotypical handsome man of your culture. How about the stereotypical beautiful woman?

READING TWO

➤ BEFORE YOU BEGIN

1. Judging from the title "Fat Is Beautiful," what do you predict this reading will be about?

2. What is your response to the title?

3. If you were going to get married one year from now, is there anything about your appearance that you would try to change (for example, lose weight)?

> ►AS YOU READ

Read "Fat Is Beautiful" through quickly one time, looking for the main idea.

FAT IS BEAUTIFUL
by Ann M. Simmons (from *The Los Angeles Times*)

1   Margaret Bassey Ene currently has one mission in life: gaining weight. The Nigerian teenager has spent every day since early June in a "fattening room" specially set aside in her father's mud-and-straw house. Most of her waking hours are spent eating bowl after bowl of rice, yams, plantains, beans, and gari, a porridge-like mixture   5
of dried cassava[1] and water. After several more weeks of starchy diet and forced inactivity, Margaret will be ready to reenter society bearing the traditional mark of female beauty among her Efik people: fat.

2   In contrast to many Western cultures where thin is in,[2] many people in the Efik and other communities in Nigeria's southeastern   10
Cross River state see a woman's fatness as a sign of good health, wealth, and beauty.

3   The fattening room is at the center of a centuries-old rite of passage[3] from girlhood to womanhood. The months spent in pursuit of weight are supplemented by daily visits from older women who   15
impart advice on how to be a successful wife and mother. "The fattening room is like a kind of school where the girl is taught about motherhood," said Sylvester Odey, director of the Cultural Center Board in Calabar, capital of Cross River state. "Your daily routine is to sleep, eat, and grow fat."   20

4   Like many traditional African customs, the fattening room is facing pressure from Western influences. Health campaigns linking excess fat to heart disease and other illnesses are changing the eating habits of many Nigerians. City people are opting out of the time-consuming process. It's an expensive process, too. Effiong Okon Etim, an Efik   25
village chief in the district of Akpabuyo, said some families cannot afford to constantly feed a daughter for more than a few months. That compares with a stay of up to two years, as was common earlier this

---

[1] *cassava:* a tropical plant with edible roots
[2] *"thin is in" (idiom):* to be thin is fashionable
[3] *rite of passage:* a special activity or ceremony used to mark the time when a person reaches a certain age, for example, becomes an adult

century, he said. But the custom continues partly because "people might laugh at you because you didn't have money to allow your child to pass through the rite of passage," Etim said. What's more, many believe an unfattened girl will be weak or unable to have children.

5   As for how fat is fat enough, there is no set standard. But the unwritten rule is the bigger the better, said Mkoyo Edet, Etim's sister. "Beauty is in the weight," said Edet, a woman in her 50s who spent three months in a fattening room when she was seven. "To be called a 'slim princess' is bad. The girl is fed constantly whether she likes it or not."

6   In Margaret's family there was never any question that she would enter the fattening room. "We inherited it from our forefathers;[4] it is one of the customs we must continue," said Edet Essien Okon, 25, Margaret's stepfather and a language and linguistics graduate of the University of Calabar. "It's a good thing to do; it's an initiation rite."[5] His wife, Nkoyo Effiong, 27, agreed: "As a woman I feel it is proper for me to put my daughter in there so she can be educated."

7   Margaret, an attractive girl with a cheerful smile, needs only six months in the fattening room because she was already naturally plump. During the process, she is treated as a goddess, but the days are monotonous. To amuse herself, Margaret has only an instrument made out of a soda bottle with a hole in it, which she taps on her hand to play traditional tunes. Still, the 16-year-old says she is enjoying the fattening practice. "I'm very happy about this," she said, her belly already falling over the waist of her skirt. "I enjoy the food, except for gari."

8   Every culture has its tradition of a beautiful bride, but what is considered beautiful varies around the world. "In order to be considered married here in Nigeria, you have to be married in the traditional way," said a woman of the Efik tribe who got married seven years ago. "Tradition identifies a people. It is important to keep up a culture. There is quite a bit of beauty in our marriages." And for the beautiful Efik bride, tradition means being as fat as possible.

---

[4] *forefathers:* ancestors (such as grandparents, great-grandparents, and so forth)

[5] *initiation rite:* similar to rite of passage, but especially for marking the joining of a new group, for example, a new community or job

➤ GETTING THE MAIN IDEA

Read the following sentences. Which one do you think expresses the author's main idea?

1. _____ For many Nigerian girls, gaining weight is considered beautiful and a necessary preparation for marriage.

2. _____ The custom of the fattening room in Nigeria is losing popularity.

3. _____ The custom of the fattening room in Nigeria is a form of discrimination against women.

➤ VOCABULARY IN CONTEXT

Find each word or phrase in the paragraph indicated in brackets [ ]. Determine the meaning of the word from the sentences. Circle the best definition.

1. in pursuit of [3]   **a.** trying to get   **b.** trying to buy

2. supplemented [3]   **a.** added to   **b.** troubled

3. impart [3]   **a.** hide or take away   **b.** give or make known

4. excess [4]   **a.** too little   **b.** too much

5. opting out [4]   **a.** deciding against   **b.** staying with

6. monotonous [7]   **a.** exciting   **b.** boring

➤ READING SKILL : Paraphrasing by Changing Grammar

The first step to paraphrasing is replacing difficult words with simple words. But in order to show that you really understand the meaning, you also need to change the word order and grammar. If you can express the meaning of the original sentence with *your own vocabulary* and *your own grammar*, you almost certainly understand the meaning.

Original: Margaret Bassey Ene <u>currently</u> has one <u>mission</u> in life: <u>gaining weight</u>. [1]

Paraphrase Step One: Replace difficult words with simple words.

Margaret Bassey Ene at the moment has one goal in life: getting fat.

Paraphrase Step Two: Change grammar.

At the moment, getting fat is Margaret Bassey Ene's life goal.

➤ READING SKILL PRACTICE ONE: Recognizing Good Paraphrases

Choose the paraphrase that most closely matches the original meaning.

1. Most of her waking hours are spent eating bowl after bowl of rice, yams, plantains, beans, and gari, a porridge-like mixture of dried cassava and water. [par 1]

   In other words,

   a. She eats rice, yams, plantains, beans, and gari, a kind of cassava porridge, all day long.

   b. She tries to stay awake by eating rice, yams, plantains, and beans so she can finally eat gari, the cassava porridge which she likes.

   c. In the morning after she wakes up she eats two bowls of rice, yams, plantains, beans, and gari, a kind of cassava porridge.

2. The fattening room is at the center of a centuries-old rite of passage from girlhood to womanhood. [par 3]

   In other words,

   a. In the middle of the 100-year-old passageway in the women's house is the fattening room.

   b. The most important thing in the traditional preparation for becoming a woman is the fattening room.

   c. The fattening room is in the middle of the old passage from girlhood to womanhood.

3. As for how fat is fat enough, there is no set standard. But the unwritten rule is the bigger the better. [par 5]

   In other words,

   a. Everyone believes women should become as big as possible, although there is no official rule about how fat they should be.

   b. It is enough to be fat, because there is no official standard, but the unofficial rule is getting bigger.

   c. Unofficially, women are better if they are bigger than the set standard.

4. During the process, she is treated as a goddess, but the days are monotonous. [par 7]

In other words,

    a. During the experience, she must worship the goddess, or her life will become boring.

    b. The process of becoming a goddess is monotonous.

    c. Although the experience is boring, she lives as richly as a goddess.

➤ READING SKILL PRACTICE TWO: Write Your Own Paraphrase

Write a paraphrase of the following sentences. First, replace the difficult words with easier words. Then complete Step Two by changing the grammar, expressing the original idea *in your own way*.

1. Original: After several more weeks of starchy diet and forced inactivity, Margaret will be ready to reenter society bearing the traditional mark of female beauty among her Efik people: fat. [par 1]

    Your paraphrase: _____

    _____

2. Original: The months spent in pursuit of weight are supplemented by daily visits from old women who impart advice on how to be a successful wife and mother. [par 3]

    Your paraphrase: _____

    _____

➤ TAKING A CLOSER LOOK

Read the article again more carefully, this time focusing on details. Decide if the following sentences are true (**T**) or false (**F**). Underline the sentence or phrase that supports your answer.

1. _____ Margaret Ene hopes to lose weight before her wedding.

2. _____ The fattening room is a new fashion in Nigeria.

3. _____ Efik people consider the fattening room as part of a young woman's education.

4. _____ One reason that the time spent in the fattening room is much shorter these days is because of the expense.

5. _____ Many Efik worry that a fat girl will be sickly or unable to have children.

6. _____ Margaret really likes the fattening room.

7. _____ Tradition is important in Efik marriages.

➤ COMMUNICATE: Values Clarification

The following is a list of twelve basic values. According to your personal point of view, rank them from 1 (most important to you) to 12 (least important). Then share your ranking with a group of three or four students.

Rank	Value	Rank	Value
_____	Health	_____	Hobbies
_____	Comfort	_____	Career
_____	My own beauty	_____	Love
_____	Other's (e.g., my partner's) beauty	_____	Friendship
_____	Time	_____	Nice house
_____	Money	_____	Nice car

Use the following expressions in your group discussion.

Asking an opinion	Expressing Personal Beliefs	Expressing Surprise
Which one did you rank as number1?	I believe . . . is most important because . . .	Really?
How about you?	I think . . . is least important because . . .	Is that so?
	I ranked . . . as number . . . because . . .	I'm surprised.
	I don't know why, but I believe that . . . is important.	

➤ INTERACTIVE JOURNAL RESPONSE

Choose one of the following questions and write a response. Be prepared to give an oral summary of your written response in small groups.

1. Were you surprised by this reading? Why or why not? What do you think about the tradition of the fattening room?

2. Are there any beauty customs from your culture that are unhealthy or uncomfortable? Describe them.

3. What are your beliefs about beauty? Have you changed your ideas after reading this chapter? Why or why not?

WIRELESS TECHNOLOGY

The development of wireless technology, such as the cell phone, has prompted innovative ways of conducting business, transmitting information, and organizing daily life while on the move.

READING ONE

➤ BEFORE YOU BEGIN

1. How has the cell phone changed the way people communicate? Do you think it is necessary to own a cell phone? Why or why not?

2. Read the title of Reading One and look at the picture. What is the man doing? Why do you think a cell phone might be useful for his business?

3. Skim the first paragraph. What new information did you find out about this man? What do you think this reading will be about?

➤ AS YOU READ

Read "Tourism Goes Wireless" quickly one time. Look for the main idea.

TOURISM GOES WIRELESS
by Puy Kea (from *Kyodo News*)

1   These days doing business is all about communication. And one of the fastest and most effective ways to do it is on the move. At least that's the reasoning behind a new business 5 venture[1] called Cyclo Tour Co. An enterprising[2] Cambodian and his French backer[3] are combining high-tech cell phones and old-tech cyclos in the hope of attracting more tourists to take the slow road through the Cambodian capital.   10

2   Cyclo Tour Co. (CTC) plans to offer cyclo tours of Phnom Penh's most famous sites. The cyclos will be decorated in the royal fashion, popular in the 1800s when the *trishaw*—a three-wheeled, human-powered bicycle—was the latest thing in personal transport. And to make it easy for riders to hail a cyclo, all the drivers will be equipped 15 with cell phones, allowing them to "speed" off to pick up customers anywhere in the capital. The cell phone numbers will be prominently

---

[1] *venture:* project
[2] *enterprising:* creative, having the ability to think of new things
[3] *backer:* someone who gives financial support

displayed in tour offices, Internet cafes, restaurants, and other areas around the city to provide quick and easy access to a mode of transport that was used back in the days when the French ruled 20 Cambodia.

3   "Motor dups," small motorcycles that haul passengers sitting sidesaddle[4] behind the driver, largely replaced cyclos years ago. Although they can be very dangerous, they are much faster than human-powered cyclos. Chea Sokhom, 60, a housewife, said she 25 vastly prefers riding in a cyclo to perching on the back of a motor dup because a cyclo is much less likely to get in a traffic accident. "Motorbikes drive very fast, while cyclos drive much slower," she explained.

4   Cyclos, which first appeared in Cambodia in the early 1800s, have 30 lost the fashionable status they once had, but Bou Sarin, who manages CTC, is seeking to bring back a colorful past with his retrofashion[5] "taxis." CTC's light, red cyclos feature seats covered in royal-design fabrics and the cell phone-equipped drivers all pedal under a banyan leaf-shaped green canopy. The combination makes 35 CTC's cyclos a vast improvement on the dingy brown or green cyclos that are only used these days to haul fruit and vegetables through crowded city streets on market days.

5   Costing $200 each, CTC's ten cyclos represent a fairly large investment for 27-year-old Bou Sarin and his French backer, but he 40 hopes both the company and the drivers, who will all be able to converse at least a little in a foreign language, will become a major attraction for Phnom Penh sightseers. The company also plans to install audio players on the cyclos so tourist sites can be explained in the tourist's own language, by experts. 45

6   To qualify as an operator, all drivers must have prior experience as cargo or passenger cyclo operators and must pass tests on traffic rules before joining CTC's fleet. Drivers will wear red T-shirts, dark blue shorts, athletic shoes, and a dark red cap. At $5 an hour, CTC's cyclos are not the cheapest transport in the city, but they are perhaps 50 destined to become the most colorful.

7   Hok Chanthy, 25, a CTC driver already selected, said he is pleased with his new job. "I am happy to be a cyclo driver because I can

---

[4] *sidesaddle*: sitting sideways on the back of a motorbike
[5] *retro-fashion*: return to the fashion style of earlier years

practice my English with foreigners every day," he said. "When our new cyclo model was first launched, some foreigners even thought *55* my cyclo belonged to the king or to the royal family. They didn't realize it was for hire." said Hok Chanthy, who has been a cyclo driver since he came to Phnom Penh in 1994 from his home in Kompong Chain Province 125 kilometers east of the capital. Prior to joining CTC, Hok Chanthy hired a normal dingy-colored cyclo from *60* a different owner to make his daily living and to get some money to study English and acquire other skills.

8   Bou Sarin, the CTC manager, said his company is already planning to expand into Siem Reap Province, where Angkor Wat and other ancient temple ruins are located, to give tourists there a similar *65* chance to leisurely see the sites in royal comfort. Travel Agencies both in Phnom Penh and Siem Reap Province are excited about Cyclo Tour Company. They believe this new high-tech operation is exactly what is needed to attract tourists in the twenty-first century.

➤ GETTING THE MAIN IDEA

Read the following statements. Which one do you think best expresses the main idea of this reading?

1. _____ Riding a cyclo in Phnom Penh is much safer than riding a motorbike.

2. _____ Tourists want high tech-tech holidays in Phnom Penh.

3. _____ Cyclo Tour Co. is a new high-tech operation hoping to attract tourists.

➤ VOCABULARY IN CONTEXT

Find each word or phrase in the paragraph indicated in brackets [ ]. From the context, guess the meaning. Then circle the best definition.

1. hail [2]   **a.** to call someone   **b.** to complain to someone

2. prominently [2]   **a.** very proudly   **b.** noticeable, easy to see

3. dingy [4]   **a.** broken   **b.** dark, old

4. converse [5]   **a.** talk   **b.** argue

5. install [5]   **a.** put in   **b.** make stronger

6. launched [7]   **a.** added to   **b.** started

➤ TAKING A CLOSER LOOK

Read the following sentences. Circle a, b, or c to fill in the blanks for each sentence. Then scan the article to check your answers.

1. Cyclos are also called _____.

    a. motor dups

    b. trishaws

    c. motor bikes

2. Cyclos are powered by _____.

    a. people

    b. cell phones

    c. motors

3. Cyclo Tour Co. is being supported with money from _____.

    a. tourists

    b. a French source

    c. a Cambodian restaurant

4. All CTC drivers will have _____ so they can be contacted from anywhere in the city.

    a. audio players

    b. Internet cafes

    c. cell phones

5. It will cost _____ per hour for the cyclo transport service.

    a. $2.00

    b. $5.00

    c. $10.00

6. Drivers must _____ to qualify as a cyclo operator for CTC.

    a. pass a driver's test

    b. own a cyclo

    c. speak fluent English

7. _____ will be put on cyclos so tourists can learn about tourist sites in their own language.

    a. a green canopy

    b. an Internet service

    c. audio players

➤ READING SKILL: Notetaking

Notetaking is an important strategy that helps you understand and remember the important information you read. Notetaking involves two steps: underlining key words and making marginal notes.

Part A: Underlining Key Words

Underlining key words means marking only the words and phrases you think are most important. Only after you have carefully read the article to determine the main ideas and supporting details should you begin to underline. Use the following steps for underlining:

1. Read the article one section at a time; for example, from heading to heading, or from the beginning of a paragraph to the end. Do not underline as you read, but mark only the sections or paragraphs containing relevant information.

2. Then begin underlining:

    • First, underline the main idea of the section or paragraph

    • Next, look for details. Do not include every detail. Be selective. Underline **only** the key words or phrases of the details you choose.

    • Finally, circle special terms or new names.

Look at the following example taken from paragraph 2 of the reading. The main idea and key words and phrases are underlined. The special term *trishaw* is circled.

Example

Cyclo Tour Co. (CTC) plans to offer cyclo tours of Phnom Penh's most famous sites. The cyclos will be decorated in the royal fashion, popular in the 1800s when the trishaw—a three-wheeled, human-powered vehicle—was the latest thing in personal transport. And to make it easy for riders to hail a cyclo, all the drivers will be equipped with cell phones, allowing them to "speed" off to pick up customers anywhere in the capital. The cell phone numbers will be prominently displayed in tour offices, Internet cafes, restaurants, and other areas around the city to provide quick and easy access to a mode of transport that was used back in the days when the French ruled Cambodia.

➤ READING SKILL PRACTICE: Underlining Key Words

Go back to the article and read paragraph 4. Then look at the list below and choose; (a) six words or phrases you would underline as key words; (b) one special term you would circle. Now mark paragraph 4 using the information you have chosen. Compare your choices with a partner.

a. *Key Words/Phrases*

red cyclos	early 1800s	Bou Sarin
manager of CTC	bring back	seats in royal-design fabric
green canopy	cell phone	CTC's cyclos
vast improvement	fruits and vegetables	market days

b. *Special Terms*

taxis	CTC's

➤ READING SKILL: Notetaking

Part B: Making Marginal Notes

Making marginal notes is the second step in notetaking. Marginal notes are written in words and phrases, not complete sentences. After you have underlined the key words and phrases of a section, go back and make marginal notes beside the section. Do not write the exact words you have underlined, but use the paraphrasing skills you learned in Unit 7 to re-phrase the marked information.

In the following example taken from paragraph 5 of the reading, the key words are underlined. There are no special terms to be circled. Marginal notes are written beside the section.

Example

Costing <u>$200 each</u>, CTC's <u>ten cyclos</u> represent a fairly <u>large investment</u> for 27-year-old Bou Sarin and his French backer, but he hopes both the company and the drivers, who will all be able to converse at least a little in a foreign language, will become a major <u>attraction for</u> Phnom Penh <u>sightseers</u>. The company also plans to <u>install audio players</u> on the cyclos so tourist <u>sites</u> can be <u>explained</u> in the <u>tourist's own language</u>, by experts.

-10 cyclos at $200 each

-big investment but will hopefully attract sightseers.

-audio players explain sites in tourist's language

► **READING SKILL PRACTICE: Making Marginal Notes**

Part A

Go back to the article and read paragraph 6. Then look at the list below and choose: (a) eight words or phrases you would underline as key words; (b) four marginal notes. Now underline and make marginal notes in paragraph 6 using the information you have chosen. Compare your choices with a partner.

a. *Key words and phrases*

driver	qualify	prior experience	pass tests
traffic rules	red T-shirt	blue shorts	athletic shoes
red cap	$5 an hour	not the cheapest	colorful

b. *Marginal notes*

driver must have prior experience	pass traffic tests
driver wears red and blue sports outfit	costs $5/hr
not very cheap	colorful way to see the sights

Part B

Read the last paragraph. Then mark it, making sure to choose only the most important words and phrases. Now write marginal notes beside the paragraph.

Compare your underlining and marginal notes with others in your class. Although some of the words and phrases you choose to underline may differ from those of your classmates, the main points of your marginal notes should be similar.

➤ COMMUNICATE: Class Survey

Which wireless devices or gadgets do your classmates have? What ones do they want? Which ones do they think are unnecessary? Use the chart below to interview your classmates.

1. Think of three other wireless devices or gadgets and write them in the chart below.

2. Then interview your classmates. Put a check (✓) in the chart to indicate their responses. Be sure to add any interesting comments they have.

Wireless devices	have one	want one	no need for one	comments
cell phone				
radio				
PDA (personal digital assistant)				

3. Add up the responses to find out which device is the most popular and which is the least popular. Discuss your findings and write them on the board.

Use the following expressions when conducting your survey.

Opening Remarks	Conducting the Survey	Closing Remarks
Do you mind if I ask you some questions? No problem, what would you like to know?	Do you have a _____? Would you like a _____? What do you think about _____? How about a _____? Do you think you need a _____? Do you want to comment?	Thanks for your information. Thanks for talking with me. I found your comments interesting, thanks!

➤ INTERACTIVE JOURNAL RESPONSE

Choose one of the following questions and write a response. Be prepared to give an oral summary of your written response in small groups.

1. While wireless technology holds promise, it takes a creative person to develop a business idea such as CTC. What do you think of the CTC business concept? Do you think the business will be a success? Why or why not?

2. Bou Sarin, CTC's company manager, is only 27 years old. Do you think it is possible for young people to develop a business in your country? Why or why not?

3. What would you like to do with technology in the future? For example, are you interested in setting up an e-business or exploring a technology-related career? Explain your ideas.

READING TWO

➤ BEFORE YOU BEGIN

1. Look at the picture. What are some of the wireless devices the people in the picture are wearing? Why do you think they might want to wear them?

2. Do you have any of these devices? If not, would you like to have any? Why or why not?

3. Now quickly read the first sentence of each paragraph. What do you think this reading will be about?

➤ AS YOU READ

Read "Wireless Wearables" through quickly one time, looking for the main idea.

WIRELESS WEARABLES
by Stefan Theil (from *Newsweek*)

1   Ted Starner first started wearing his computer in 1993. He would strap a shoe box of electronics to his waist and a small keyboard to his wrist and then put on a bulky headset with a small display monitor suspended in front of his left eye. After a while the other students at the Massachusetts Institute of Technology stopped staring at him   5 and accepted him as just another nerd.[1] Nowadays, however, Starner is looking much more fashionable. He's a professor at Georgia Tech in Atlanta, for one thing, and his wearable computer looks just like

---

[1] *nerd:* someone who is a technological expert but is socially unskilled

a pair of ordinary black-rimmed glasses—except for the thumb-sized gadget on the frame that beams a tiny, bright image onto the lens.   10

2   What used to be big clunky devices only a nerd could love have now become miniature in size. Thanks to the high-tech fashion industry, computers can now be built into almost any piece of clothing or accessory. The idea is to have the computer disappear into your clothes so that no one knows you have it.   15

3   Today, high-tech companies together with clothing firms are putting miniature computers into everything from watches to running shoes. They are wireless and can be linked to each other and to the Internet. An American company, for example, has inserted a microphone into a necklace, speakers into a pair of earrings, and a   20
mouse under the stone of a ring. And a Japanese company is bringing out a wearable, wireless Internet device with a lightweight headset that lets you walk, talk, and surf the Web at the same time.

4   Although these up-to-date fashions sound interesting, some people may wonder what exactly they are supposed to do with all this   25
wearable technology. The introduction of always-on, wireless devices will let people communicate, interact, get information and entertainment wherever they go, all the time. Companies developing this high-tech fashion envision always-on e-mail, "buddy alerts" that sense if your friends are nearby, plus downloadable music and videos   30
wherever you go. Computers will remind you to do things, tell you if you're about to forget your keys at home, and guide you through a world in which everything is "smart" and gives out information.

5   Staying in tune with all that requires more than a handheld device, claim analysts at high-tech companies who are developing wireless   35
fashion. They estimate that by 2010, 40 percent of adults and 75 percent of teenagers will wear always-on devices. They predict that for every hour people spend in the real world, they'll spend ten in the "e-world."

6   Companies are targeting today's teenagers as early adopters of   40
wearable technology. Already one company has developed a running shoe with a built-in wireless pedometer that tracks speed and distance. Teens who have tested the shoe say it's "right on"[2] as a sports training shoe and really "cool"[3] to wear on the streets. Another company is

---

[2] *right on:* perfect
[3] *cool:* very fashionable

developing high-tech fabrics that turn clothes into sensors—clothes   45
that alert the wearer when friends are nearby or when parents are
approaching to check up on homework. Teens say sensors that can
relay this kind of information are bound to be big sellers.

7   But before these devices become popular, engineers will have to   50
resolve a few technical issues. First, wireless technology will have to
be made reliable enough to support always-on devices. Second,
wearable devices will need to be less expensive. The first wearables
on the market will cost anywhere from $1,700 U.S. to $7,000 U.S.
That's way too expensive for the majority of teens. Finally, to make   55
the environment "smart," a new kind of communication network
will need to be developed. This will involve connecting every shop or
product to big servers that direct the flow of information to these
high-tech fashion devices. But that's not likely to be up and running   60
any time soon.

➤ GETTING THE MAIN IDEA

Read the following statements. Which one do you think best expresses the
author's main idea?

1. _____ Soon we will all be wearing wireless computers wherever we go.

2. _____ Companies are developing fashions that show off high-tech wireless
devices.

3. _____ Clothing and accessories will soon be developed into high-tech fashions.

➤ VOCABULARY IN CONTEXT

The following list of words can be found in the reading passage. Scan each paragraph indicated in brackets [ ] to find the word. Read the sentence where the
word is found to guess its meaning from context. Then use the words to complete the sentences.

bulky [1]   suspended [1]   envision [4]

adopters [6]   resolve [7]   reliable [7]

1. Young people are usually the first _____ of new fashions.

2. I do not trust the information in the magazine; it is often not _____.

3. The two friends tried to _____ their disagreement by discussing the matter alone.

4. The model airplane was _____ from the ceiling.

5. The equipment was so _____ we could not carry it, so we used a cart to move it.

6. She must be very creative to _____ such an interesting idea for the company.

➤ TAKING A CLOSER LOOK

Read "Wireless Wearables" again, this time focusing on details. Decide if the following sentences are true (**T**) or false (**F**). Underline the sentence or phrase which supports your answer.

1. _____ Ted Starner does not know much about technology.

2. _____ Wireless devices cannot be sewn into clothing.

3. _____ You will not be able to use the Internet with these new wireless devices.

4. _____ The purpose of a "buddy alert" is to find music files on the Internet.

5. _____ "Smart" computer devices will give you advice and information through the day.

6. _____ Probably more adults than teenagers will wear wireless fashions.

7. _____ High-tech fashions will be very expensive when they first come on the market.

8. _____ Shops will be able to contact the wireless device directly in the future.

➤ READING SKILL: Notetaking

Notetaking forces you to think about what you have just read and helps you to separate important from nonimportant information. Review the steps for note-taking from Reading One (pages 114–116) to help you complete the following exercises.

►READING SKILL PRACTICE: Notetaking

Part A

Go back to Reading Two and read paragraph 3. Then look at the list below and choose: (a) four words or phrases you would underline as key words; (b) one special term; (c) two marginal notes. Now mark paragraph 3 using the information you have chosen. Compare your choices with a partner.

a. *Key Words*

high-tech companies   clothing firms

miniature computers into everything from watches to running shoes

wireless and can be linked to each other and the Internet

microphone into a necklace   speakers into a pair of earrings

Japanese headset that lets you walk, talk, and surf the Web at the same time

b. *Special Terms*

wireless   Internet   Web

c. *Marginal Notes*

wireless fashions developed by U.S. and Japanese high-tech companies and clothing firms

microphone into a necklace

Japanese headsets

can be linked to each other and the Internet

speakers into a pair of earrings

Part B

Now read the rest of the article and mark it. Remember to be selective; not every paragraph needs to be marked. Compare your underlining and marginal notes with others in your class. Although some of the words and phrases you choose to underline may differ from those of your classmates, the main points of your marginal notes should be similar.

➤ COMMUNICATE: Designing a Wireless Device

Work in small groups.

Design a wireless wearable device you think might be popular with students in your class. Make a sketch of the device and write brief notes on what it is and how it works. Then explain your device to your classmates.

Use the following expressions when explaining your design to your classmates.

Introducing the device	Explaining how the device works
We'd like to introduce our design to you.	First you ...
	Then you ...
Please look at ...	
	You can use it by ...
This is a ...	

➤ INTERACTIVE JOURNAL RESPONSE

Choose one of the following questions and write a response. Be prepared to give an oral summary of your written response in small groups.

1. Do you think it is important to have access to the Internet all the time? Why or why not?

2. According to the reading, companies are marketing wireless wearable devices aimed at teenagers. Do you think this is a good marketing strategy? Why or why not?

3. Some people say high-tech devices are interfering with traditional face-to-face interaction. Do you agree? Why or why not? Do you think society will benefit from the introduction of high-tech wearable devices? Why or why not?

4. In some societies cell phones and various other wireless devices have been banned from use in public places and while driving. Do you agree with this ban? Why or why not?

MEDIA AND CULTURE

M edia bring the global village into our own living room. We can turn on our television or open up the newspaper and see the whole world at a glance. How do media affect culture? How have media from the industrialized world affected the cultures

READING ONE

➤ BEFORE YOU BEGIN

1. When you were a child, what was your favorite TV program? Why?

2. What foreign television shows or movies have been popular in your culture? Why?

3. Fill out the chart by guessing the English word for each machine.

machine to take pictures	camera
machine to tell the time	
machine to make fire	
machine to travel from place to place	
machine to talk with someone far away	

➤ AS YOU READ

Now read "People from Mars" quickly one time. Look for the main idea.

PEOPLE FROM MARS

by Helena Norberg-Hodge (from *Ancient Futures: Learning from Ladakh*)

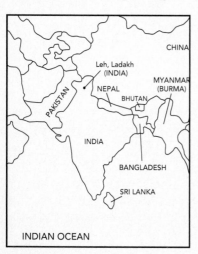

1   Imagine suddenly waking up to find your town invaded by people from another planet. Speaking a strange language and looking even stranger, these extraterrestrials[1] lead quite ⁵ amazing lives. They do not appear to know what work is, but enjoy constant leisure. Moreover, they have special powers and inexhaustible wealth. This is how tourists appeared to the ¹⁰ traditional villagers of Ladakh—like people from Mars!

---

[1] *extraterrestrials:* people coming from outside of the Earth, from other planets

2   I was in Ladakh from the time tourism started and was able to observe the process of change from the beginning. Since I spoke the language fluently, I gained an insight into the strong psychological pressures that modernization brings. When I looked at the modern world from something of a Ladakh perspective, I also became aware that our culture looks much more successful from the outside than we experience it on the inside.

3   Each day, the tourists from "another world" would spend as much as a hundred dollars each, the same amount that a Ladakhi family might spend in a year. This would be roughly equivalent to someone spending fifty thousand dollars a day in America. Ladakhis did not understand the role that money played for the foreigners. In the traditional subsistence economy[2] of Ladakh, money had played a minor role, used primarily for luxuries—jewelry, silver, and gold. Basic needs—food, clothing, and shelter—were provided for without money. The labor one needed was free of charge, part of the web of human relationships. But back home the tourists needed money to survive. In their modern societies, food, clothing, and shelter all cost money—a lot of money.

4   Compared to these strangers, the Ladakhis suddenly felt poor. During my first years in Ladakh, young children I had never seen before used to run up to me and press apricots into my hands. Now children in worn-out Western clothing greet foreigners by holding out an empty hand. They demand, "One pen, one pen," a phrase that has become the new mantra[3] of Ladakhi children.

5   Development has brought not only tourism to Ladakh, but also Western and Indian films and more recently, television. Together they provide images of luxury and power. There are countless magical machines—machines to take pictures, machines to tell the time, machines to make fire, to travel from one place to another, to talk with someone far away. Machines can do everything for you; it is no wonder the tourists look so clean and have such soft hands. In films, the rich and the beautiful have lives filled with excitement and glamor.[4] For the young Ladakhis, the picture is irresistible.

---

[2] *subsistence economy:* an economy which is just enough to supply the bare necessities of life

[3] *mantra:* a Hindu or Buddhist religious prayer that is repeated again and again

[4] *glamor:* attractive and exciting qualities

6   By contrast, they begin to think their own lives seem primitive. The TV view of modern life becomes a slap in the face.[5] They feel stupid and ashamed. They are asked by their parents to choose a way   50 of life that involves working in the fields and getting their hands dirty for very little or no money. Their own culture seems absurd compared with the world of the tourists and film heroes.

7   For millions of youths in rural areas of the world, modern Western culture appears far superior to their own. All they can see is the   55 material side of the modern world—the obvious wealth of Western culture. They cannot so readily see the social or psychological problems—the stress, the loneliness, the fear of growing old. Nor can they see environmental problems, inflation,[6] or unemployment. On the other hand, they know their own culture inside out, including all   60 its limitations and imperfections. They take for granted the peace of mind and the warm family and community relations of their village.

8   The Western influence has caused some Ladakhis—the young men in particular—to develop feelings of inferiority.[7] They reject their own culture, and at the same time eagerly take on the new one. They run   65 after the symbols of modernity: sunglasses, Walkmans, and blue jeans several sizes too small—not because they find those jeans more attractive or comfortable but because they are symbols of modern life.

9   Modern symbols seem to have also contributed to an increase in aggression in Ladakh. Now young boys see violence glamorized on   70 the screen. From Western films, they can easily get the impression that if they want to be modern, they should smoke one cigarette after another, get a fast car, and race through the countryside shooting people left and right.

10   It has been painful to see the changes in my young Ladakhi   75 friends. Of course they do not all turn violent, but they do become angry and less secure. I have seen a culture change—a culture in which even young men used to be happy to cuddle a baby or to be loving and soft with their grandmothers.

---

[5] *a slap in the face:* an insult

[6] *inflation:* an increase of prices and a fall in the value of money

[7] *inferiority:* being lower in ability or importance

➤ GETTING THE MAIN IDEA

Read the following sentences. Which one do you think best expresses the author's main idea?

1. _____ Ladakhi culture has been negatively affected by tourism and Western TV and films.

2. _____ Ladakhis can learn about the reality of Western culture by meeting tourists and watching TV and films.

3. _____ Primitive Ladakhi culture should become modernized, so the influence of wealthy tourists and Western television is necessary.

➤ VOCABULARY IN CONTEXT

Find each word or phrase in the paragraph indicated in brackets [ ]. From the context, guess the meaning. Then write the meaning in the space provided. Finally, use a dictionary to check your accuracy.

1. leisure [1]

   Your guess from context: _____

   Dictionary: _____

2. inexhaustible [1]

   Your guess from context: _____

   Dictionary: _____

3. equivalent [3]

   Your guess from context: _____

   Dictionary: _____

4. irresistible [5]

   Your guess from context: _____

   Dictionary: _____

5. absurd [6]

Your guess from context: _____

Dictionary: _____

6. symbols [8]

Your guess from context: _____

Dictionary: _____

7. cuddle [10]

Your guess from context: _____

Dictionary: _____

►TAKING A CLOSER LOOK

Scan "People From Mars" for the answers to the following questions. Decide if the following sentences are true (**T**) or false (**F**). Go back to the reading and underline the sentence or phrase that supports your answer. Compare your answers with a partner.

1. _____ In one day, a tourist would spend the same amount a Ladakhi family might spend in a year.

2. _____ In a traditional subsistence economy, money plays an important role.

3. _____ In earlier times, Ladakhi children would give the author gifts of food.

4. _____ Young Ladakhis think Americans are silly and primitive.

5. _____ Young Ladakhis usually do not see problems of stress and loneliness on American TV programs.

6. _____ The young men of Ladakh want to wear sunglasses and blue jeans to imitate American culture.

7. _____ Since television and Western films have been shown in Ladakh, there has been a decrease in aggression and violence.

8. _____ The author thinks that in traditional Ladakhi society, young people were more willing to give attention to babies and grandparents than they are today.

➤READING SKILL: Outlining

In Unit 8 you learned the reading strategy of notetaking—underlining, circling, and making marginal notes. After notetaking, it can be helpful to organize the main ideas in an outline. By making an outline, you can understand and remember the reading more easily. In an outline, you group the facts according to the main topics and ideas you have found.

Outline Model

    I. Heading (Topic)

        A. Subheading (more specific category)

        B. Subheading (more specific category)

        C. Subheading (more specific category)

            1. Examples or details

            2. Examples or details

   II. Heading

        A. Subheading

        B. Subheading

            1. Examples or details

            2. Examples or details

        C. Subheading

➤READING SKILL PRACTICE: Outlining

1. Go back and read "People from Mars" again, this time making notes by circling, underlining, or writing marginal notes.

2. The outline on pages 132–133 is for Reading One, "People From Mars." Fill in the outline by choosing from the list at the toof page 132. You will need to look back at the reading and your marginal notes.

> violence, aggression
>
> want symbols of Western culture
>
> machines used by tourists and on TV
>
> see attractive materialism of Western culture
>
> traditionally, money plays minor role
>
> environmental problems, inflation, unemployment

Effects of tourism, Western films, and television on Ladakh

   I. Comparison between Ladakhi subsistence economy and tourist economy

        A. Tourists spend equivalent of $50,000 a day

        B. _____

        C. Compared to tourists, Ladakhis feel poor.

  II. Images of luxury and power in tourists and on TV

        A. _____

        B. TV and film show modern Western life

            1. Exciting, beautiful

 III. Comparison between Ladakhi lifestyle and Western media lifestyle

        A. Young Ladhakis feel their lives are foolish

        B. _____

        C. Can't see negative social/psychological problems

            1. Stress, loneliness, old age

            2. _____

  IV. Effects on young Ladakhis

        A. Inferiority

        B. Reject own culture, embrace new one

C. _____

   1. Sunglasses, Walkmans, blue jeans

   2. _____

   3. Smoking, driving, shooting

D. Become angry and less secure

►COMMUNICATE: Media Analysis

1. At home, watch a TV program for 30 minutes. Take notes on four of the people or characters.

Name of Program					
Type of program					
Name of Person / Character	Gender	Profession / Role	Age	Social Class	Race
1.					
2.					
3.					
4.					

What image does this program present of society? Consider male-female ratio, age, profession, social class, race, happiness, ways of spending time, and so forth. Do you think it matches reality?

_____

_____

_____

Are there any signs of environmental, social, or emotional problems in the program?

_____

_____

_____

2. In class, describe your research to a small group.

3. After everyone in your group has shared, decide if there were any similarities. Your teacher may ask you to report to the class.

Use the following expressions as you share your research.

Sharing Research	Clarifying
From my research, I found that . . .	Did you say . . . ?
From this program, it seems that . . .	Could you repeat that please?
I was surprised/not surprised to see that . . .	Do you mean . . . ?
Responding	**Coordinating Information**
How interesting/surprising!	My research shows similar/different things.
Really?	
I'm not surprised to hear that.	I have one similar example.
	My research is quite different.

➤ INTERACTIVE JOURNAL RESPONSE

Choose one of the following questions and write a response. Be prepared to give an oral summary of your written response in small groups.

1. Do you tend to believe the news as it is shown on TV or in the newspaper? Why or why not?

2. What do you think about the situation in Ladakh as described in Reading One? Do you believe everything the author reports?

3. Can you think of any solution to the problems described in "People from Mars?"

4. What are some good influences of the media?

READING TWO

➤ **BEFORE YOU BEGIN**

1. Before families had televisions at home, how did children spend their free time? List your ideas in the space below.

_____   _____   _____

_____   _____   _____

2. In your opinion, does television have a positive influence on children or a negative influence? Share your ideas with a partner.

➤ **AS YOU READ**

Now read "The Role of Television in Inuit Culture" quickly one time, looking for the main idea.

THE ROLE OF TELEVISION IN INUIT CULTURE

1   Until the 1970s, the Inuit[1] people of Northern Canada led isolated and traditional lives, untouched by modern media and high technology. In 1973, the arrival of TV via satellite introduced the Inuit to "southern" (Canadian and U.S.) culture. Watching television became a popular way to pass the long, dark Arctic nights. From the point of   5
view of the Inuit, the results were mixed.

2   Before 1973, life in a typical Inuit village largely revolved around family and neighbors. Children went to school during the day to learn basic arithmetic and language skills, including the study of Inuktitut, the traditional language of the Inuit. Inuktitut has been   10
spoken for thousands of years, but it has only been written in recent years. After school and on weekends, young people learned hunting and fishing skills from their elders. Of course they did not learn only hunting skills, but also important values. For example, values such as sharing and cooperation were necessary for survival in the harsh   15
northern environment.

3   But in 1973, along came the first of Canada's Anik satellites, and life in Northern Canada changed drastically. Children learned

---

[1] *Inuit:* native people of Northern Canada (used to be known as "Eskimo")

English but started to lose their own Inuit language. Young people quickly picked up new ideas, new values, and new attitudes from television. Some of these were a challenge to the old ways; for example, the focus on individual materialism and ownership in TV ads and game shows contradicted the traditional importance given to cooperation. Work and school attendance and time spent hunting and fishing dropped. Young people didn't want to learn hunting and fishing skills from their elders anymore. As one Inuit elder said, "When television first came, the effect of television on the community was very drastic. People no longer visited their neighbors. Children did not play outside, and the interactive activities of the community in general were broken down. The home and the family was the last refuge of the Inuit language. Television, by coming into the home, was invading this last refuge."

4   In this situation, we might expect the traditional culture to be completely lost when faced with modern information. But because so many Inuit, especially the older people, were concerned about the effects of TV on their culture and language, they chose another way: As an experimental solution, the Inuit Broadcasting Corporation was created in 1982 to provide TV programs in the local language. When the mainstream CBC (Canadian Broadcasting Corporation) saw the popularity of local-language programming, it began to change its programming to meet the needs of the multilingual and multicultural audience. Throughout the 1980s, the north's many aboriginal[2] languages were heard more and more on CBC in its programs for the North. Taqravut, an Inuktitut-language program produced in Montreal and Ottawa, became popular. In 1992, Television Northern Canada began broadcasts in ten native languages to 94 small communities in the North. These networks produced about six hours a week of programming in their language, Inuktitut: current affairs, drama, and a children's series which uses animation and puppets to teach Inuit history and culture. But these were all weekly programs, and if Northerners wanted daily news, they had to turn to the South. Finally, in 1995, 40 years after the first TV screen flickered to life in the North, CBC North TV went daily. Northern TV news, gathered in the North, produced in the North, about the North, became

---

[2] *aboriginal:* existing from earliest times, or from before the arrival of colonists

available every weekday to the 65,000 people of the Northwest Territories and the 31,000 people of the Yukon.

5   Native broadcasting in northern Canada has been successful: 85 percent of Inuit viewers over the age of 9 watch 1 to 3 hours a week of the native programs in their own language that relate to their own   60 experience, and new jobs have been created. This Inuit project has shown that TV is a powerful force that can be used to support their culture if they keep control: "One of the purposes of our television project was to use television to understand ourselves, to remember our past, but also to broaden our horizons. We want to use television   65 not only to protect our language and culture but as a means of artistic expression." It is estimated today that by the age of 18, most Inuit will have watched 30,000 hours of TV, twice the time spent by the average Canadian teenager. Although the global village has invaded the homes scattered across the northern reaches of Canada, traditional   70 cultures and languages are at the same time being respected and, indeed, developed.

➤ GETTING THE MAIN IDEA

Read the following sentences. Which one do you think expresses the author's main idea?

1. _____   The Inuit led isolated lives before the arrival of TV in 1973.

2. _____   Inuit culture was negatively affected by English TV.

3. _____   It is possible to use TV to support, rather than change, traditional culture.

➤ VOCABULARY IN CONTEXT

Find each word or phrase in the paragraph indicated in brackets [ ]. From the context, guess the meaning. Then write the meaning in the space provided. Finally, use a dictionary to check your accuracy.

1. revolved [2]

   Your guess from context: _____

   Dictionary: _____

2. contradicted [3]

Your guess from context: _____

Dictionary: _____

3. drastic [3]

Your guess from context: _____

Dictionary: _____

4. refuge [3]

Your guess from context: _____

Dictionary: _____

5. flickered [4]

Your guess from context: _____

Dictionary: _____

6. broaden [5]

Your guess from context: _____

Dictionary: _____

➤ TAKING A CLOSER LOOK

Scan "The Role of Television in Inuit Culture" for the answers to the following questions. Decide if the following sentences are true (**T**) or false (**F**). Go back to the reading and underline the sentence or phrase that supports your answer. Compare your answers with a partner.

1. _____ All Inuit people hate English TV because it has so many bad effects on their children.

2. _____ Inuit children found it difficult to learn English from television.

3. _____ Some traditions of the Inuit, like hunting and visiting one's neighbors, declined after the arrival of TV.

4. _____ In order to limit the influence of English TV on their culture, the Inuit created their own TV broadcasts in their own language.

5. _____ Inuit children are now not allowed to watch any English TV.

6. _____ The average Canadian teenager watches twice as much TV as Inuit teenagers.

➤ READING SKILL PRACTICE: Outlining

The following is an outline for "The Role of Television in Inuit Culture." Turning back to the reading, do the following:

1. Read and underline or highlight key words.

2. Write marginal notes.

3. Using your highlighted words and marginal notes, fill in the missing words or phrases in the outline.

"The Role of Television in Inuit Culture"

    I. Traditional lifestyle of Inuit before the 1970s

        A. Revolved around family and neighbors

        B. Children learned

           1. Went to school to study Inuktitut

           2. _____

           3. _____

  II. _____

        A. _____

           1. Learned English

           2. _____

           3. _____

        B. Other effects of TV

           1. Work and school attendance droped

           2. _____

3. _____

III.

A. Inuit Broadcasting Corporation 1982—local language

B.

C.

D.

E. Success—85 percent of viewers over age of 19 watch 1 to 3 hours of native TV

► COMMUNICATE: Class Survey

1. By yourself, make up a yes/no question to find out your classmates' opinions about media and culture. Then interview your classmates by asking them your yes/no question. Count the yes and no responses, and take notes on any interesting comments that they add.

Question	Yes	No	Classmates' Comments
Do you think that English language movies have affected other cultures?	10	5	I think it depends on the individual viewer. Yes, they do, and it can't be helped. No, I don't believe that movies are so powerful. Yes. I enjoy learning English from watching foreign movies.

Your question: _____

_____

2. Meet with a small group and share your results.

Use the following expressions as you discuss your survey results.

Sharing Survey Results	Clarifying	Responding
From my survey, I found that . . .	Did you say . . . ?	How interesting/surprising!
		Really?
It seems that most classmates . . .	Could you repeat that please?	I'm not surprised to hear that.
I was surprised/not surprised to see that . . .	Do you mean? . . .	

3. Your teacher may ask your group to report to the class.

➤ INTERACTIVE JOURNAL RESPONSE

Choose one of the following questions and write a response. Be prepared to give an oral summary of your written response in small groups.

1. What impact do you think foreign media has had on the young people in your culture? Consider fashion, music, food, and social values.

2. What image of your culture would an Inuit or Ladakhi have if he watched local TV from your country?

3. What is your opinion of the Inuit attempt to protect their language and culture through media? Do you think it will continue to be successful in the future? Why or why not?

DEVELOPMENT

Many of us believe that to be rich is to be happy. We spend a lot of time working to make money to buy the high-tech, convenient things we love to use and throw away. We often feel sorry for people in our own culture and in other countries who seem to be less "developed" than we are. What is development? Is it possible for everyone to have a high quality of life and still protect the environment?

READING ONE

➤ BEFORE YOU BEGIN

1. In a small group, brainstorm words that you think are connected to a developed country, and to a developing country.

   Developed Country   **Developing Country**

   <u>small families</u>   <u>large families</u>

   _____   _____

   _____   _____

   _____   _____

2. In a small group, rank these countries from most developed to least developed: India, Mexico, France, Canada. Rank them based on <u>one</u> criterion. "Criterion" means your standard of judging: the way you measured the ranking. For example, one criterion might be years of education per citizen.

   Criterion for ranking: _____

   Your Group's Ranking

   1. _____

   2. _____

   3. _____

   4. _____

3. When your group is ready, your teacher will write the group criteria and rankings on the board. Is there agreement about the rankings? Could a list of all the criteria be considered a good definition of development?

➤ AS YOU READ

Read the article "What Is Development?" quickly to get the main ideas.

WHAT IS DEVELOPMENT?

1   Even though the word "development" is used every day in the newspapers and on television, there are many different meanings depending on who is speaking. For some experts, development means becoming industrialized like the United States or Japan. The economy of an industrialized country can be measured in terms of the growth of the Gross National Product (GNP). Other experts like to define development in political terms, that is, how a society establishes goals to implement economic change. And some see development as a certain "quality of life," which might include such things as health care, education, leisure time, and so forth. Indeed, there are still other variations on the definition of development, as this short article will present.

2   "Development" has most generally meant the level of industrialization of a country. Until only a few years ago, industrialization was considered by many to be the end point of the development process. A common way to measure development is by the Gross National Product (GNP); that is, rating nations by their economic level by comparing the total value of goods produced in one year. When countries are ranked by their economic level, they fall into two general groups: the developed countries (industrialized countries) and the developing countries (industrializing countries). About 70 percent of the world's population lives in developing countries, also known as Third World countries. Located in Asia, Africa, and Latin America, these countries have low levels of industry and per capita income[1] and low rates of economic growth.

3   However, dividing the world into these two parts may be simplistic and misleading.[2] Take India, for example. Because of its low GNP, India is considered a developing country, but it could be said that India is quite developed in its long, complex history and culture. For instance, it is the birthplace of Hinduism and Buddhism, major world religions. It has an old, sophisticated[3] medical tradition, "Ayurveda," which Western science today is just beginning to research. These are just some ways in which India is highly developed.

---

[1] *per capita income:* average salary for each person
[2] *misleading:* giving the wrong impression of something
[3] *sophisticated:* complicated, high-level

Other more industrialized countries may look like babies compared to this "grandmother of human development."   35

4   So there are other ways to measure the level of development of a country. A recent definition of development has included the quality of life of the country's citizens, based on such things as health care, education, leisure time, life expectancy, and buying power. The Human Development Index (HDI) is a new measure of development   40 which was made by the United Nations to use instead of GNP to compare the development of the world's countries. It combines three criteria: Gross Domestic Product (GDP) per person, adult literacy[4] rate, and life expectancy.[5]

5   But even using the HDI as a way of measuring a country's devel-   45 opment ignores a very important problem. That is, while highly industrialized countries may have a high economic level, literacy rate, and life expectancy, they usually suffer a problem that is growing more serious every year: environmental pollution. The pollution of our seas, air, and land decreases our quality of life by   50 affecting our health. More serious is the future possibility of the end of the earth and human life itself. We may become so "developed" that we kill ourselves! Therefore, the most recent definition of development emphasizes sustainable[6] development: the improvement of human quality of life within the limits of a green, healthy Earth.   55 In other words, development which tries to protect, not destroy, the earth's resources, so that our present lifestyle does not harm future generations' lifestyles.

6   If real development means that a society provides a high level of economic, physical, intellectual, and spiritual life to each citizen   60 while protecting the health of the Earth, then no country is perfectly "developed" yet. Industrialized and industrializing nations can learn from each other's cultures and traditions about the best ways to build a high-level, sustainable quality of life for everyone. It can be said that both industrialized and industrializing nations are in a period   65 of transition, with many different hopes for the future. Many in the industrialized world support a new "postindustrial" society, where knowledge, information, and space-age technologies are important. Others don't like the idea of an impersonal high-tech society and

---

[4] *literacy:* the ability to read and write
[5] *life expectancy:* estimated lifespan (how long the average person lives)
[6] *sustainable:* able to support or keep going

believe that the "greening" of society—an appreciation for nature, 70
human community, and sustainable economics—should become the
new goal of development. Meanwhile, there are still the age-old
tragedies of hunger, disease, war, and social and political cruelties
that continue worldwide despite our attempts at so-called development.

►GETTING THE MAIN IDEA

Read the following sentences. Which one do you think best expresses the
author's main idea?

1. _____ There are many ways to define and measure development.

2. _____ There are two common ways of defining development.

3. _____ Development often destroys the environment.

►VOCABULARY IN CONTEXT

Find each word or phrase in the paragraph indicated in brackets [ ]. From the
context, guess the meaning. Then write the meaning in the space provided.
Finally, use a dictionary to check your accuracy.

1. establishes [1]

   Your guess from context: _____

   Dictionary: _____

2. implement [1]

   Your guess from context: _____

   Dictionary: _____

3. simplistic [3]

   Your guess from context: _____

   Dictionary: _____

4. combine [4]

   Your guess from context: _____

   Dictionary: _____

5. transition [6]

Your guess from context: _____

Dictionary: _____

► TAKING A CLOSER LOOK

Complete these sentences using information from the reading. Compare your answers with your classmates.

1. Three definitions of development mentioned in the first paragraph are:

    _____.

2. "Development" generally refers to the _____.

3. Gross National Product is _____.

4. _____ percent of the world is considered "developed."

5. The author claims that India could be considered "developed" because

    _____.

6. The Human Development Index tries to measure _____

    _____.

7. Using GNP and HDI as a way to measure development ignores the problem

    of _____.

8. The purpose of sustainable development is to _____

    _____.

► READING SKILL: Summarizing

To "summarize" means to state the main idea and important supporting points of a reading in a shorter, simpler way. A summary is much more general than the original passage. Making a summary of a newspaper article or a chapter from your textbook helps you to understand the main idea and also to remember it. Sometimes a teacher may check on your comprehension of a reading by asking you for a written or oral summary.

Steps in Summary Writing:

1. Read carefully, underlining key words and phrases, and writing marginal notes as you learned in Unit 8.

2. Make an outline from your marginal notes as you learned in Unit 9.

3. Write the summary in your own words, using your outline as a guide. Remember to paraphrase difficult language in your own words. The summary should be simple and easy to understand.

➤ READING SKILL PRACTICE: Summarizing

1. Using your marginal notes, fill in the outline below and on page 150.

2. Then, using the outline, fill in the missing information to complete the summary on page 150.

The Outline

What is Development?

    I. Introduction: three views of development

        A. Industrialization (economic)

        B. _____

        C. Social (quality of life)

    II. Most common meaning of development: industrialization

        A. Measured by GNP

        B. Two groups

            1. _____ (industrialized)

            2. Developing (_____)

    III. Problem with using GNP: simplistic

        A. Example of India

            1. Developed in _____ and medicine

IV. HDI

    A. Quality of life

    B. _____, literacy rate, _____

  V. Problem with HDI

    A. Ignores _____

VI. Solution — _____

    A. Quality of life which does not destroy the Earth

VII. Conclusion—Goals in the Time of Transition

    A. Postindustrial high-tech

    B. _____

The Summary

"What Is Development?"

This reading discusses the definitions and ways to measure development.
Generally, development means the _____, measured by
(1)
_____ (GNP). Based on this, countries can be divided into two
(2)
groups: _____ (industrialized) and _____ (industrial-
(3)   (4)
izing). However, GNP does not measure cultural development such as religion
and medical knowledge, so that even though India is highly developed culturally,
it is considered a _____ country. Another way of measuring devel-
(5)
opment is by the _____ (HDI) which tries to measure the
(6)
_____ by considering three factors; GDP per person, literacy rate,
(7)
and _____. However, this measurement _____ the
(8)   (9)
environmental cost of development. Finally, the article suggests that development should be judged by its _____. This means achieving a high
(10)
quality of life which does not destroy the environment.

COMMUNICATE: Creative Thinking

1. In your small group, look at the following three rankings. In each list, the countries have been ranked from the most developed to the least developed according to one criterion. Try to guess what this criterion is. Hint: It might help to think about what the leading country is famous for, or especially good at.

Ranking A India Criterion of Development: _____

Mexico

France

Canada

Ranking B India Criterion of Development: _____

Canada

Mexico

France

Ranking C Canada Criterion of Development: _____

France

Mexico

India

2. After each group shares its ideas with the class, add to the list of criteria for measuring "development" that you made in (Before You Begin) on page 144. In your opinion, is your country a "developed" country? Why or why not?

Offering suggestions/ hypothesizing	Responding to Suggestions
It could be . . .	Good idea!
It might be . . .	That's possible.
Perhaps it's . . .	I think so, too.
How about . . .?	Interesting suggestion!
I've got it! It's . . .	It's an interesting suggestion, but . . .

➤ **INTERACTIVE JOURNAL RESPONSE**

Choose one of the following questions and write a response. Be prepared to give an oral summary of your written response in small groups.

1. What is your definition of development?

2. Which country in the world do you consider to be the most developed?

3. Would you like to live there? Why or why not?

4. In what ways do you wish your own country were more developed?

5. In your opinion, is "sustainable development" possible for your country? For the world?

READINGS TWO AND THREE

➤ **BEFORE YOU BEGIN**

After considering the following questions, talk about your hometown to a partner.

1. Did you grow up in a city, town, or village, or the country? What were the good points and bad points of your hometown? Consider all areas of "development": economic level, politics, health, education, leisure, pollution, and so on.

2. Imagine what your hometown will be like in 50 years. Will it be the same, worse, or better? Why?

➤ **AS YOU READ**

Your teacher will assign you Reading Two or Reading Three. As the first step of this exercise, you will read your assigned article and write an outline and summary of it. As the second step, you will be telling your partner the summary of your reading and listening to your partner explain his or her summary.

Now read your assigned article once quickly to get the main idea.

READING TWO

NOTHING WASTED, EVERYTHING GAINED
by Alan Weisman (from *Gaviotas: A Village to Reinvent the World*)

1   The rush to the cities was one of the global trends of the twentieth century. In the beginning of the century, only 14 percent of the world's population lived in cities. By the end, the majority of the population lived in cities, and these cities were overcrowded and polluted. The twenty-first century

faces a population crisis, and specialists from a variety of fields from engineering to agriculture are meeting to create more sustainable living environments outside of the major urban areas. Gaviotas, a rural area in Colombia, is an example of how even desolate[1] places in the countryside can be developed for sustainable human use.

2   This area of Colombia had been considered a wasteland: dry brown savanna,[2] without enough water, plant, or animal life to support a town. But today as one approaches the town, a green spot appears on the brown horizon, and big aluminum sunflowers begin to dot the empty savanna. As it turns out, the green spot is a 25,000-acre forest and the sunflowers are windmills.

3   Under the trees are low white buildings and colorful houses, all with solar collectors.[3] Begun in 1971 as a scientific experiment, Gaviotas is now a self-sufficient[4] town of 200, supported by clean, renewable industries. A handful of Colombian engineers and soil chemists were the first to settle in Gaviotas. They were persuaded by

---

[1] *desolate:* empty, with no sign of life or comfort
[2] *savanna:* a flat, grassy area with few or no trees
[3] *solar collectors:* devices for gathering and storing energy from the sun
[4] *self-sufficient:* able to provide for one's needs without outside help

a Colombian visionary[5] named Paolo Lugari to try to make an unlivable place livable. Lugari predicted that by the twenty-first century, expanding populations would have to live in "unlivable" places. He wanted to see if it would be possible to restore the unproductive savanna to a place where humans could live well.

4   The first problem was finding pure water. The Gaviotans invented a special kind of hand pump to reach deepwater reservoirs. They developed solar heaters to use the sun's energy to clean the drinking water and soil-free hydroponic[6] systems to raise food. These inventions have spread to other parts of Latin America; nearly 700 villages in Colombia alone now use the pumps developed in Gaviotas.

5   Another goal was to restore the soil[7] and plants. After years of experimentation, Gaviotas scientists discovered that Caribbean pines from Honduras could grow in the area's thin, acidic soil. At the same time, resin from the trees could be tapped without cutting down the forest, and used in paints, cosmetics, perfumes and medicines.

6   Besides providing a sustainable living, the pines have also created what biologists call a miracle: After several years of healthy growth, a 25,000-acre tropical forest developed on the once dry savanna. Soon animal life such as deer and hawks were seen. The 250 plant species identified so far have been studied in the Gaviotan's research lab for possible medicinal uses.

7   As more people moved to Gaviotas, it was important to consider a pollution-free way of transportation. Village mechanics developed a bicycle especially designed for the area's rough land. Bicycles are now the official mode of transportation, cheap and pollution-free.

8   Gaviotas is a remarkable accomplishment of sustainable development. This once dry landscape has been turned into a near paradise.

---

[5] *visionary:* person who has the imagination to see future possibilities
[6] *hydroponic:* soil-free way of growing plants in special water
[7] *soil:* the top layer of earth in which plants grow

➤ GETTING THE MAIN IDEA

Read the following sentences. Which one do you think best expresses the author's main idea?

1. _____ The Gaviotas project shows that people can develop an environment in a sustainable way.

2. _____ Energy from the sun can be used by humans for many different purposes.

3. _____ It is important to find pollution-free kinds of transportation for urban centers.

➤ TAKING A CLOSER LOOK

Complete these sentences using information from the reading. Then compare your answers with other students who read about Gaviotas.

1. We need to learn how to make "unlivable" places livable because _____

   _____ .

2. Before 1971, the area of Gaviotas was _____ .

3. Gaviotas was started as an _____ by the visionary

   _____ .

4. Energy is made by _____ and _____

   _____ .

5. Food is grown in _____ _____ .

6. The creation of a _____ _____ is considered a

   miracle because _____ .

➤ READING SKILL PRACTICE: Summarizing

1. Reread the passage carefully, underlining key words and phrases and writing marginal notes.

2. Make an outline on page 156 using your marginal notes.

3. Write a summary using your outline. Be sure to use your own words in a clear, simple way.

4. When you are finished, you can compare your summary with a student who also read about Gaviotas.

The Outline

The Summary

_____

_____

_____

_____

READING THREE

THE MOST INNOVATIVE CITY
by Robin Wright (from *The Los Angeles Times*)

1   Problems such as poverty,[1] crime, and pollution are common to many of the world's cities. But Curitiba, Brazil, a city of 1.6 million people, is different. It is a good model of sustainable urban development.

2   Like most other overcrowded and poor cities in the world, Curitiba had a serious garbage problem until it introduced its "garbage that is not garbage" program. Through this program, more than 70 percent of its trash is recycled—compared with 25 percent in Los Angeles. Christano Pinheiro, a seven-year-old boy, shows how it's done. At the start of the school year, Pinheiro traded eight pounds of recyclable garbage for a packet of new notebooks. Each week, he and his two older brothers exchange trash for fresh fruit or two pounds of protein-rich beans. Curitiba is now known as the world's recycling capital.

3   Household garbage was not the only reason to begin a recycling program. Old worn-out equipment was frequently being replaced with new technology. Like every other city, old yet usable materials were being dumped around the city. This gave engineers and architects an opportunity to work together to use the materials creatively. Old wooden telephone poles are now reused in office buildings, bridges, and public squares. Retired buses have become mobile[2] classrooms for adult education. "Virtually everything has more than one use," said Mayor Rafael Greca, whose airy office overlooking a park is made from old poles and glass. "It's just a matter of figuring out how to reuse things and then teaching people how to do it."

4   Environmental efforts were only a small part of the plan for Curitiba. The latest additions are the Lighthouses of Learning, based on the great lighthouse and library in Alexandria, Egypt. The first Lighthouse was built as an experiment in 1995 to determine exactly who would use it, and the effect it would have on the neighborhood. Within six months of being opened, it was clear that it was popular. Soon after, a Lighthouse was built in each of the city's neighborhoods.

[1] *poverty:* the state of being poor (having little money)
[2] *mobile:* moveable

The brightly colored Lighthouses have 5000-volume libraries on the first floor, reading rooms on the second, and a guard in a light tower that transmits[3] a strong beam to provide community security. "One of the Lighthouses is near my home, so I use it for all my school projects," said Deucina Costa, a high school senior who stops in every few weeks. "So do my 10-year-old brother and 12-year-old sister. Mom lets them come because it's safe." The Lighthouses have cut crime rates. They each cost about $180,000. "It's cheaper to build libraries than prisons," said Greca.

5   Curitiba is also taking government to the people. Unlike other cities where government buildings are located in an often isolated, expensive area, government offices in Curitiba are accessible[4] to everyone on what is known as Citizen Streets. These Citizen Streets are colorful covered avenues of government offices and shops where residents can pay their bills, get a marriage license, have a haircut, buy groceries, or file a police report. The Citizen Streets have 600-seat open theaters, sports areas, and classrooms that offer professional training for $1 a course.

6   "We're trying to create a whole new set of attitudes and a sense of involvement in this city," Greca said. "To the people of Curitiba, this city is the best human invention there is."

---

[3] *transmit:* to send out
[4] *accessible:* able to be reached and used

➤ GETTING THE MAIN IDEA

Read the following sentences. Which one do you think best expresses the author's main idea?

1. _____ Curitiba is famous because it has so many typical problems of urban centers, including pollution.

2. _____ The changes in Curitiba have made it a more sustainable and better city to live in.

3. _____ Because the crime rate was so high in Curitiba, it was necessary to build Lighthouses for community security.

➤ TAKING A CLOSER LOOK

Complete these sentences using information from the reading. Then compare your answers with another student who read Reading 3.

1. Household garbage in Curitiba is exchanged for _____,

   _____ and _____ as part of the city's

   _____ program.

2. _____ and _____ are recycled to make buildings and classrooms.

3. The Lighthouses of Learning have two purposes: _____ and

   _____.

4. Two things you can do on Citizen Streets are _____ and

   _____.

5. The reason they made the Citizen Streets was _____.

➤ READING SKILL PRACTICE: Summarizing

1. Reread the passage carefully, underlining key words and phrases and writing marginal notes.

2. Make an outline on page 160 using your marginal notes.

3. Write a summary using your outline. Be sure to use your own words in a clear, simple way.

4. When you are finished, you can compare your summary with a student who also read about Curitiba.

The Outline

The Summary

_____.

_____.

_____.

_____.

►COMMUNICATE: Read and Tell

Now you are ready to explain your summary to a student who didn't read your article. Work with someone who read the other article. Take turns explaining to each other what your articles are about.

1. This is a speaking and listening activity, so it is important that you don't simply read your summary. Explain, don't read. Look at your outline (*not* your summary) to help you to remember, and then look up and make eye contact with your partner. Speak enthusiastically, trying to communicate with your partner.

2. If you are the listener, do not try to read the article or your partner's outline or summary. Listen actively. You may ask your partner questions.

Use the following expressions in your oral summary.

Summarizing
The title of my reading is _____ and it is about _____.
There are _____ (number) main points: _____, _____, and _____.
First (next, finally), I would like to explain _____. The author says . . .
Let's go on to the next point.
This concludes my summary of _____. Do you have any questions?

Clarifying/Checking
Excuse me, I couldn't catch what you said at the beginning (in the middle, near the end) . . . Could you repeat that please?
I'm sorry, can I check this? Does the author mean . . .?
Did you say . . .?
How do you spell that?

➤ INTERACTIVE JOURNAL RESPONSE

Choose one of the following questions and write a response. Be prepared to give an oral summary of your written response in small groups.

1. Would you like to live in Gaviotas? Why or why not? What kind of people do you suppose choose to live there?

2. In your opinion, what was the most innovative change in Curitiba? Explain your answer.

3. Do you have an innovative idea that might improve your city? Describe it.

4. If you could design a perfect city, what would its main features be?

CLONING

Cloning—using genes or genetic information from cells of one animal, plant, or human to create an exact copy of the original—is one of the most popular fields of research these days. Already, cloned animals exist, and many of us have been eating genetically modified food for some time now. Some say it is just a

READINGS ONE, TWO, AND THREE

➤ BEFORE YOU BEGIN

1. Work in a small group. Ask the following survey questions about genetic engineering. Then compile the answers of all your classmates on the board.

Is it acceptable to:	Student 1	Student 2	Student 3	Student 4
clone animals?	Yes/No	Yes/No	Yes/No	Yes/No
clone humans?	Yes/No	Yes/No	Yes/No	Yes/No
genetically alter farm produce?	Yes/No	Yes/No	Yes/No	Yes/No

2. Look at the results of your class survey. Is there agreement on any of the questions? Ask several of your classmates to give reasons for their answers.

➤ READING SKILL: Summary Presentation

Your teacher will ask you to join Group 1, Group 2, or Group 3. Your group will be given one news article to read, take notes on, summarize, and present.

Step One

1. Read the article by yourself one time.

2. Complete the exercises that follow your assigned article to check your understanding.

Step Two

1. Read the article again, this time underlining, highlighting, and making marginal notes on the main ideas and supporting details.

2. Make an outline using your marginal notes.

3. Compare your outline with others in your group to make sure you have all the information.

4. Write the summary using your outline as a guide. Remember to paraphrase difficult language in your own words. When you are finished, you can compare your summary with those of others in your group.

Step Three

Join a new group with students who read the other two articles. Explain the main points of your summary. Do not read the information directly from your summary. Use your outline to help you. Remember to make eye contact with your group members as you speak. When you have finished, make sure to ask if there are any questions.

Use the following expressions as you give your oral summary.

Summarizing
The title of my article is _____ and it is about _____.
There are _____ (number) main points: _____, _____, and _____.
First (next, finally), I would like to explain _____.
The author says . . .
Let's go on to the next point.
This concludes my summary of _____. Do you have any questions?

Use these expressions to ask questions about a summary.

Clarifying/Checking
Excuse me, I couldn't catch what you said at the beginning (in the middle, near the end) ...
I'm sorry, can I check this? Does the author mean . . . ?
Did you say . . . ?
How do you spell that?

Step Four

After listening to your classmates' summaries of the other two articles, turn to page 176. Check your understanding of the three articles by taking the quiz. Then do the Interactive Journal Response on page 177.

Group 1

READING ONE

DOLLY'S CREATORS CLONE PIGS
(from the *Associated Press*)

1   PPL Therapeutics, which cloned Dolly, said today that five healthy
piglets were born March 5 in Blackburg, Virginia, U.S.A. They were
cloned from an adult pig using a slightly different technique than
the one that produced Dolly. Independent tests of the DNA of the
piglets—named Millie, Christa, Alexis, Carrel, and Dotcom—con-   5
firmed they were clones of the pig, the company said.

2   Scientists have been studying pigs for several years for potential
xenotransplantation—putting the organs of one species into
another species. The cloning might hold out hope that pigs could be
genetically engineered so that their organs or cells would be more   10
easily accepted by the human body, making it easier for them to be
transplanted. "I think this is a positive step forward they've made,"
said Dr. Fritz Bach of Harvard Medical School, who studies genetic
transplants[1] from animals to people.

3   Genetic engineering is one potential benefit, Bach said. In addition,   15
scientists could simply clone pigs that prove exceptionally well-suited
for transplants to humans, he said. But Bach stressed that ethical
issues[2] about animal-to-human transplants, mainly the risk of
introducing new germs to humans, must be solved before such
procedures are done. Imutran, a Cambridge, England-based company   20
that is pursuing similar research, called PPL's announcement
"interesting news." The company said, "It's potentially a useful
technology to develop new lines of pigs for [transplant], however,
the next step is to see if the technology can be applied to developing
genetically modified animals whose organs can be transplanted into   25
humans without being rejected."

4   PPL, based in Edinburgh, Scotland, said transplantation of
genetically altered pig organs could be tested on humans in the near

---

[1] *transplant:* a surgical operation in which a diseased or missing part of a person's
body is replaced by another person's (or animal's) body part
[2] *ethical issues:* concerns arising from a system of moral beliefs about what is right and wrong

future and that analysts believe the market for them could be worth $6 billion.

5   PPL scientists plan to try to remove a gene in pig cells so that the transplanted pig organ will not be rejected in the human body. In place of this gene, three new genes will then be introduced into the pig cells, and the transplant patient would receive a blood transfusion containing modified cells taken from the pig supplying the organ. Scientists hope this process will allow for successful transplants between pigs and humans.

6   The idea of xenotransplantation, however, has a long and varied history. Scientists were dabbling in the area well before the first successful human-to-human transplants. In 1905, a French surgeon tried unsuccessfully to transplant a rabbit kidney into a young girl, and medical history books are sprinkled with even earlier failed operations.

7   As a general rule, baboons were considered the best animals to use for the transplants because of their similarity to humans. Organs from other animals were swiftly rejected—sometimes even before the transplant operation was completed. As soon as human blood starts flowing through the animal organ, the immune system[3] begins to reject it. Within a matter of minutes blood clots form, literally starving the organ of oxygen. In 1984, an experiment using xenotransplantation captured world attention. Surgeons at Loma Linda University Medical Centre in California put a young baboon heart into a 14-day-old girl known as Baby Fae, who was born with a fatal heart defect. The child lived for only 20 days after surgery. Results like this in the past have created controversy over the possibility of pig transplantation. But scientists are excited by the prospect of using animal organs for transplant because of the shortage of human organs. Many people die while waiting for a transplant. Scientists are now eager to experiment in the hope that pigs will be able to provide a steady supply of organs. "We have high hopes that an end to the chronic organ shortage is now in sight," a PPL representative said.

8   The names of the first cloned piglets each have their own importance. Millie was named for the millennium. Christa, Alexis, and Carrel were named after Dr. Christiaan Barnard, who performed the

---

[3] *immune system:* antibodies (substances) produced in the blood which help to protect against disease

first human heart transplant, and Dr. Alexis Carrel, who won the   65
Nobel prize in 1912 for his work in the field of transplantation.

9   And as for Dotcom . . . " anyone can guess where that name
comes from."

➤ GETTING THE MAIN IDEA

Check the statement you think best expresses the main idea of this reading.

1. _____ The idea of animal transplants is creating concern for many people.

2. _____ The birth of five piglets is raising hopes for xenotransplantation.

3. _____ Human immune systems reject the organs of animals.

➤ VOCABULARY IN CONTEXT

Find each word or phrase in the paragraph indicated in brackets [ ]. From the context, guess the meaning. Then write the meaning in the space provided. Finally, use a dictionary to check your accuracy.

1. pursuing [3]

   Your guess from context: _____

   Dictionary: _____

2. rejected [3]

   Your guess from context: _____

   Dictionary: _____

3. altered [4]

   Your guess from context: _____

   Dictionary: _____

4. prospect [7]

   Your guess from context: _____

   Dictionary: _____

5. chronic [7]

   Your guess from context: _____

   Dictionary: _____

►TAKING A CLOSER LOOK

Answer the following questions to check your understanding of Reading One.

1. What is xenotransplantation?

2. What is the main ethical issue connected with animal-to-human transplants?

3. What steps are scientists taking to try and solve this ethical issue?

4. What other kinds of animal-to-human transplants have been carried out in the past? How successful have they been?

5. Why are scientists excited about the possibility of pig transplantation?

Group 2

READING TWO

TO CLONE OR NOT TO CLONE: IMPLICATIONS OF HUMAN CLONING
by Ian Wilmu (from *Time*)

1   In the excitement after the birth of Dolly, most scientists declared that Dolly should not create fears—that there would be no interest in using the technology to clone people. But already they are being proved wrong. There has been an enormous change in attitude, as scientists have become interested in the notion of   5
cloning and, in particular, cloning a human being. Some infertility[1] centers that said they would never clone now say they are considering it. A handful of fertility centers around the world are conducting experiments with human eggs that lay the basis for cloning, and more and more scientists and doctors now claim it will just be a   10
matter of time before the first human is cloned.

_____

[1] *infertility*: the inability to produce babies

2   But up until now, the procedure has been very difficult. The basic problem is that cloning is a very inefficient procedure. The incidence of death among fetuses[2] and offspring[3] produced by cloning is much higher than it is through natural reproduction—roughly ten times as high as normal before birth and three times as high after birth. But even if the technique were perfected, scientists must ask why would people want to "copy" people in the first place, and what the consequences might be.

3   Most likely, couples that are infertile might choose to have a copy of one of them rather than accept genes[4] from an unknown donor. Each of us can imagine the difficulties that could result from the introduction of a cloned child. For example, it would be very difficult for the parent that was cloned not to have specific ideas about how the "copy" (the cloned child) should act and develop. Seeing their own image would make it awfully difficult not to impose expectations upon their cloned child. Conversely, how would the cloned teenager react to the parent, seeing their physical future ahead?

4   Another case for cloning might be to bring back a child who died or was killed tragically. Any parent can understand that wish, but it must be first recognized that the copy would be a new baby and not the lost child. Herein lies the difficulty, for the grieving parents are seeking not a new baby but a return of the dead one. Since the original would be fondly remembered as having particular talents and interests, would not the parents expect the copy to be the same? It is possible, however, that the copy would develop quite differently. Is it fair to the new child to place it in a family with such unnatural expectations?

5   "Copy" is also suggested as a means by which parents can have the child of their dreams. Couples might choose to have a copy of a film star, baseball player, or scientist, depending on their interests. But because personality is only partly the result of genetic inheritance, conflict would be sure to arise if the cloned child failed to develop the same interests as the original. What if the Einstein shows no interest in science? Or the football player turns to acting?

---

[2] *fetuses:* unborn humans or animals in the later stages of development

[3] *offspring:* children

[4] *gene:* a part of a cell in a living organism which controls physical characteristics, growth, and development. Genes can reproduce themselves and are passed on from one generation to another

6   To add to the problems associated with designing a dream clone, scientists still know very little about cloning in terms of aging. The British researchers who cloned Dolly the sheep have discovered that she is growing old before her time. Researchers suspect that it is because Dolly was cloned from a 6-year-old sheep. At present, researchers predict that Dolly will die of natural causes before her chromosomes[5] claim them, but that might not be the case with human cloning.

7   There are various reasons to advance the technology for human cloning, but there are also many problems that surround the issue. At present there is a large effort involved in learning more about the human genome[6] and the biology associated with cloning. It is hoped the time required for this research will provide an opportunity for societies and individuals to decide how they wish the technique to be used.

---

[5] *chromosomes*: the parts of cells that contain the genes
[6] *human genome*: the set of chromosomes that contains the genetic information of human beings

➤ GETTING THE MAIN IDEA

Check the statement you think best expresses the main idea of this reading.

1. _____ Human cloning could only be done by rich people.

2. _____ While there are reasons for human cloning, many problems surround the issue.

3. _____ The biggest worry for scientists is how quickly the human clone will age.

➤ VOCABULARY IN CONTEXT

Find each word or phrase in the paragraph indicated in brackets [ ]. From the context, guess the meaning. Then write the meaning in the space provided. Finally, use a dictionary to check your accuracy.

1. incidence [2]

Your guess from context: _____

Dictionary: _____

   2. consequences [2]

   Your guess from context: _____

   Dictionary: _____

   3. impose [3]

   Your guess from context: _____

   Dictionary: _____

   4. grieving [4]

   Your guess from context: _____

   Dictionary: _____

   5. conflict [5]

   Your guess from context: _____

   Dictionary: _____

►TAKING A CLOSER LOOK

Answer the following questions to check your understanding of Reading Two.

   1. What was the interest in human cloning just after the birth of Dolly? How has this changed?

   2. What is the basic problem with the technique of human cloning at present?

   3. What are three cases where parents might choose to clone a child?

   4. What difficulties surround these three cases?

   5. What reason do researchers give for the aging of Dolly?

Group 3

READING THREE

CLONING OF "MAN'S BEST FRIEND"

by Matt Crenson (from www.nandotimes.com)

1   Animal cloning is a powerful way to understand life. The science of animal cloning is looked upon as a way to help improve the quality of farm animals. It is also viewed as a way to feed and clothe an expanding population. Scientists claim that animals will be engineered to produce more meat, wool, eggs, and milk. It is also recognized as a way to save some of the most endangered animals in the world from extinction.

2   Scientists have already developed a relatively simple technique to produce Dolly the sheep, the world's first "man-made" clone of an adult animal. More recently, there have been new explorations in the area of animal cloning—the cloning of man's best friend.

3   It all began when Richard Denniston of Louisiana found himself suffering the same grief that millions of other pet owners have faced: His dog, a little Scottish terrier, had a brain tumor,[1] and it would be only a matter of time before the dog died. Like most in his situation, Denniston just wanted to end the dog's pain. But he took it one step further. An expert in animal reproduction, Denniston collected a tiny skin sample from the dog and took it to his laboratory where he developed it and then froze it in liquid nitrogen. From that idea, Denniston started Lazaron BioTechnologies, a company that will save pet DNA[2] for $500, plus a monthly storage fee of $10, until cloning dogs is made possible.

4   The cost is bound to be prohibitively expensive at first, but it will eventually come down to a few thousand dollars, says Carol Bardwick, the president of Canine Cryobank in San Marcos, California. Dolly, the sheep that started it all, was the first clone ever produced from an adult animal cell. When she was born in 1997, most biologists believed that cloning was decades in the future. Since then, cattle, goats, mice, and monkeys have been cloned in labs. "I

[1] *brain tumor:* a mass of diseased or abnormal cells in the brain
[2] *DNA:* nucleic acids within cells responsible for passing specific characteristics from parents to children

really believe that the technology is going to become available for   30
many species in the near future," Denniston says.

5   Mark Westhusin, a Texas A&M veterinarian[3] and the lead
researcher of Lazaron Bio Technologies, is very confident about the
dog-cloning technique. At the moment at least four companies are
competing to develop the technology.   35

6   So far the steps leading up to the actual cloning are fairly clear. At
present, when a pet owner contacts a gene[4] bank, the bank will send
a DNA collection kit. A veterinarian performs a routine skin biopsy,[5] puts the sample in a special transport medium and sends it to the
gene bank. At the bank, the skin cells are placed in a growth medi-   40
um that causes them to divide a few times. Then they're frozen in liquid nitrogen at minus 376 degrees Fahrenheit and kept at the gene
bank until they are ready to be used.

7   Oddly enough, dog cloning may be more appropriate to lovable
mutts[6] than to high-quality purebreds, says Princeton University   45
cloning authority Lee Silver. Because mutts are born from dogs of
various breeds, an identical dog cannot be reproduced, therefore
cloning would be the only way to get anything like the original dog,
Silver says. A purebred, on the other hand, is genetically designed by
years of careful breeding[7] to come out the same every time.   50

8   Westhusin says there are still some major research issues to work out.
For example, female dogs produce only a small number of eggs once
every six months or so. That means researchers only have a few eggs
to work with.

9   But despite the implications, pet cloning is bound to become a   55
growth industry. "If you look at how attached people are to pets, this
is not an unusual situation. I'm sure lots of them would clone pets if
they knew they could," he [Westhusin] said. "Certainly some of our
customers are crazy," Hawthorne says. "But far more of them are
simply crazy about their animals."

---

[3] *veterinarian:* doctor of animals
[4] *gene:* a part of the cell made up of DNA which controls physical characteristics, growth,
and development. Genes can reproduce themselves and are passed on from one generation
to another.
[5] *biopsy:* the removal of cells from the body for the purpose of testing
[6] *mutts:* dogs of mixed breeds
[7] *breeding:* raising animals to produce new or better types

➤ GETTING THE MAIN IDEA

Check the statement you think best expresses the main idea of this reading.

1. _____ Pet lovers are very interested in the possibility of pet cloning.

2. _____ Cloning your pet is sure to be expensive and very difficult.

3. _____ Cloning will be most popular for purebred dogs.

➤ VOCABULARY IN CONTEXT

Find each word or phrase in the paragraph indicated in brackets [ ]. From the context, guess the meaning. Then write the meaning in the space provided. Finally, use a dictionary to check your accuracy.

1. extinction [1]

   Your guess from context: _____

   Dictionary: _____

2. grief [3]

   Your guess from context: _____

   Dictionary: _____

3. prohibitively [4]

   Your guess from context: _____

   Dictionary: _____

4. appropriate [7]

   Your guess from context: _____

   Dictionary: _____

5. implications [9]

   Your guess from context: _____

   Dictionary: _____

➤ TAKING A CLOSER LOOK

Answer the following questions to check your understanding of Reading Three.

1. Why do scientists believe animal cloning is important?

2. What reason did Richard Denniston have to begin research on dog cloning?

3. How are the cells of a dog collected and stored?

4. Why is dog cloning more appropriate for mutts than for purebred dogs?

5. What is one issue connected with dog cloning at present?

Students from All Groups

➤ QUIZ

After listening to your group members' presentations, take the following quiz by marking **T** (true) or **F** (false) to check your understanding of the three news articles.

1. _____ The term for animal cloning is "xenotransplantation."

2. _____ Animal-to-human transplants may be possible through the cloning of pigs.

3. _____ The problem with animal-to-human transplants at present is that the organs of animals are often rejected in the human body.

4. _____ At present there is no need for animal organ transplants because many human organs are available.

5. _____ Human cloning is very easy to do.

6. _____ A cloned child would naturally have the same interests and talents as its donor.

7. _____ The age of the donor may have some effect on the rate of aging of the copy.

8. _____ The idea of dog cloning came about when a dog owner decided it would be a good way to make money.

9. _____ Dog cells will be kept in a gene bank until they are ready to be used.

10. _____ Cloning purebred dogs will be more popular than cloning mutts.

11. _____ It will be more expensive to clone purebreds than mutts.

12. _____ It is easy to do research on dog cloning because female dogs produce many eggs all the time.

➤ **INTERACTIVE JOURNAL RESPONSE**

Choose one of the following questions and write a response. Be prepared to give an oral summary of your written response in small groups.

1. What reasons do the authors of Reading One and Reading Three give for animal cloning? After considering the reasons, do you think animal cloning is the right course of action to take? Why or why not? Has your opinion changed since beginning this unit?

2. The author of Reading Two discusses three reasons why couples might choose to clone a child. What are those reasons? Based on your personal beliefs, do you think conducting experiments on human cloning for these reasons is acceptable? Why or why not?

FUTURE WORLDS

W e often think that the future is mysterious and unknown, but isn't it true that the future is created by our present actions? It is exciting to imagine the future and consider how today's

READING ONE

►BEFORE YOU BEGIN

Part A

Read the following metaphors for the future, and circle the one that best describes your feeling about the world of tomorrow.

1. The future is a roller coaster on a moonless night.

2. The future is a mighty river.

3. The future is an ocean.

4. The future is a random dice game.

Give reasons for your choice:

_____

_____

_____

Then work with students who chose the same metaphor and compare your reasons.

Part B

Imagine this: The Earth has been almost destroyed by some disaster, like nuclear war or environmental accident. One group of survivors escapes and builds a new society called "Surreal" under the earth. The other group makes their society above ground in a country called "Laurania." Hundreds of years pass. Now you, who were born in Laurania, have the chance to meet and spend the afternoon with a person who was born in Surreal. What would you talk about?

List five questions that you would like to ask the person from Surreal.

_____

_____

_____

_____

_____

List five questions that the Surreal resident might like to ask you.

_____

_____

_____

_____

_____

Share your questions with a partner or a small group.

➤ AS YOU READ

This unit's reading is a science fiction story. Rather than skimming the story quickly as you do with an article, read it more slowly and carefully. Try to read it from the beginning to the end in one sitting. Use these questions to focus your reading:

1. Who are the main characters?

2. Where are they?

3. What happens?

4. Why did the author write this story?

LUKE IN THE FOREST
by Suzanne Martel (from *The City Underground*)

1   Luke was off on one of his dangerous adventures. Every afternoon after school, he had made his way to the open air—to the edge of the fascinating outer world. Now that he knew the way, it took him less than an hour to reach the mouth of the tunnel. He decided to venture out of the safe tunnel. He took a few steps out of the hill. Small stones flew out from under his feet and he lost his balance and rolled to the bottom of the hill.

2   Looking dizzily[1] around, he saw that he had landed near those tall, sharp-needled trees that ancient science books called pines. Putting his hand to his face, he made sure that his gas mask was secure. Above him, he could see the entrance to the tunnel in the

_____

[1] *dizzily:* off balance; confused

side of the mountain. Since he had come so far, he might as well go all the way.

3   Picking up his helmet, he started off, taking cautious little steps and stopping every minute to look at something new. The song of   15 a bird surprised him, and its quick flight was even more wonderful. The deep silence of the natural world amazed him after the mechanical sounds of a world run by motors. He touched the rough bark of a tree with wonder.

4   Suddenly, a wild cry reached his ears and he froze with fright.   20 Who lived on the surface of the earth? What terrible danger was near? He suddenly realized how far he had traveled from his protective cave. Would he die alone without anyone ever knowing what became of him? He felt frightened in his new world. He heard sounds coming closer, branches breaking—and suddenly a great   25 furry animal attacked the terrified boy and pushed him over. A long tail waved in the air, and a hot tongue licked his cheek. Luke's eyes closed, and he waited for death.

5   Finally he opened his eyes and lifted up his head as the enemy leaned over him, panting, its long tongue hanging out, its silky   30 ears framing a long-nosed face—and its dangerous tail waving about.

6   "Don't be frightened!"

7   "I'm *not* frightened." Luke answered as if it were perfectly natural for an animal to start a conversation with him.   35

8   "Your *thoughts* are frightened, though. I felt them!"

9   Luke spoke to the huge animal sitting beside him. "Then you must also know that I've stopped being frightened." At twelve, a boy has his pride and is quick to defend it.

10   "Where are you?" asked the voice. "I don't see you anywhere."   40

11   Luke answered, "I'm here in front of you—are you blind?" He felt sorry for this furry creature with the big tail who could not see something right under his nose. He continued questioning it. "Are there a lot of you on earth—where do you live?"

12   Loud laughter just behind him made him scramble to his feet,   45 ready for a new attack. But there was no enemy facing him. Instead he saw a girl with long red hair, as tall as himself, dressed in a brown dress. She was shaking with laughter.

13   "You were talking to Bark, but he can't answer you."

14   "He was very polite, though," Luke said, annoyed as the creature ran over to the newcomer and licked her hand.

15   "How funny you are," the girl said. "You have no hair, and you're wearing a mask. Did you come from the moon?"

16   Luke was too dumbfounded to answer. This was an astonishing moment. All the theories he had been taught all his life were turning out to be wrong. A world supposed to be deserted was inhabited.[2] Animals ran through it, and human beings walked in its green forests. Strangely enough, though, he felt as if he were coming back to his own land after a long absence.

17   But the girl's superior tone annoyed him, so he turned to his four-footed listener again. "Do you belong to the wolf family?" he asked politely.

18   "He won't answer you, you know," the girl said. "He's my dog, Bark." And, as if in agreement, the dog barked shortly.

19   "That's what *you* think. As a matter of fact, Bark and I had a very nice chat—before you came along."

20   The girl shook her head. "No you didn't! I was the one who was communicating with you. We were exchanging ideas by telepathy."

21   Luke was immediately interested. "Show me your apparatus,[3] then," he said—and frowned as the girl laughed at him again.

22   "There isn't any apparatus. My ideas simply flash to your brain, and yours answer them. You ought to understand because you're a telepathist yourself—and quite a good one. You communicate very clearly, even from a long distance away. And we don't even speak the same language."

23   For the first time Luke realized that this was true; when the girl spoke aloud, strange sounds came out of her mouth. But fortunately, thanks to telepathy, they could communicate even through the language barrier.

---

[2] *inhabited:* with people/animals living there
[3] *apparatus:* equipment or machinery

24   The girl flashed a friendly smile. "My name's Agatha. What's   85
yours?"

25   "Luke 15 P 9. And I live in Surreal, under the mountain." He
pointed to Mount Royal and the opening to the tunnel.

26   Agatha accepted this calmly. "I live behind the mountain, on the
bank of the river. Our tribe settled Laurania." She leaned forward   90
curiously. "Why are you wearing that mask? And what are you
doing in these woods? Bark and I often come here, but we've never
seen you before."

27   "This is the first time I've come down the mountain," Luke said. He
didn't like to explain that he was wearing a mask because the open air   95
was poisonous; he felt that such a remark might hurt her feelings. "I'm
used to synthetic[4] air—that's why I wear a mask. Now tell me what
you're doing so far from your home."

28   "My father and brother went out hunting, and I decided to pick
some blueberries." She ran to the edge of the forest and came back,   100
holding out a handful of tiny blue balls. "Here, do you want some?"

29   Luke took one politely. Raising his mask, he swallowed it without
chewing.

30   "Go on," Agatha urged, "have some more."

31   "No thanks. It's not good to take more than one pill."   105

32   Agatha went on eating berries until her mouth was stained blue.
The sight made Luke curious; he had always enjoyed getting to the
bottom of[5] things. Now he wanted to know all about these strange
blue pills.

33   "Do you find these pills ready-made?" he asked eagerly. Before she   110
could answer, he demanded, "Is that all you eat?"

34   Agatha stared at him, amazed. "Why no, of course not! We eat the
animals we catch, and fish from the river—and bread, naturally."

35   Agatha took a piece of bread out of her pocket, divided it into two,
and gave half to Luke. He examined it carefully.   115

36   "This is my snack," Agatha said, biting into it. And Luke, who had
never seen anyone eat so much in his life, feared for her health.

37   Always adventurous, he risked taking a tiny bite. But first he asked,
"What's it made of?"

38   "It's made of flour."   120

---

[4] *synthetic:* artificial, not natural
[5] *"get to the bottom of" (idiom):* to understand

39   "Flour? Where do you get that from?"

40   "From wheat, you idiot! Don't you know anything at all?"

41   Luke turned red; he did not realize that what he *did* know would amaze this girl far more than what he *didn't* know. To hide his embarrassment, he asked her another question. "Is that a hat, that fur stuff you're wearing?"   125

42   Agatha put her hand to her head as if to find out. "Of course not," she said. "Can't you see that I'm bareheaded?"

43   Luke began to remember his ancient history. "Then it must be fur, like the skins our ancestors used to wear."   130

44   But Agatha shook her head. "You really don't know much, I see," she said. "This is *hair*." And she shook her beautiful red hair.

45   Luke stared at it with surprise. "Don't you—don't you ever take it off, even when you go to bed?"

46   Agatha smiled. "No, never. Not even in summertime."   135

47   "It must be very hot," Luke sympathized. But although her hair was certainly strange, he found it rather pretty.

48   "It's no hotter than your mask. You live *under* the mountain?" Agatha said, as if the strangeness of such an idea had just struck her. "Under the *earth*?" What a strange idea!   140

49   For a long time, the two youngsters sat under the pines, comparing their different ways of life, the scientific knowledge of Surreal, with all its restrictions, and the simplicity and freedom of Laurania. Luke told her about the origin of his people, about the Great Destruction, and how the refugees from the mountain had built a magnificent underground city. He had learned all this at school. He was proud of his country.   145

50   Agatha's story was simpler. She could remember an old story about a fiery disaster and a terrible plague.[6] "The survivors made their homes in the devastated lands," she explained. "First they lived like animals. Then they formed groups and began to live in tribes so that they could help one another in storms, and against diseases and wild animals."   150

51   They didn't always understand each other clearly. Telepathy could not always cross the language barrier, and Luke's technical terms were as difficult to explain as the natural wonders that Agatha described. But the two youngsters trusted each other and accepted the most surprising ideas quite calmly.   155

---

[6] *plague*: spread of disease

52   "Well Luke, why did you decide to come out of Surreal? Weren't you afraid?"

"Oh that was just chance!" A modest[7] boy, Luke did not want to   160
53   boast about his brave adventure. "I happened to find an opening. And I—I felt drawn."[8]

"That was probably me calling you," Agatha said wisely. "I often come to this spot with Bark—and I've often wished for a friend."

---

[7] *modest:* not proud, rather shy
[8] *drawn:* pulled, attracted to

➤ VOCABULARY IN CONTEXT

Find each word or phrase in the line indicated in brackets [ ]. From the context, guess the meaning. Then write the meaning in the space provided. Finally, use a dictionary to check your accuracy.

1. venture   [1]

   Your guess from context: _____

   Dictionary: _____

2. cautious   [3]

   Your guess from context: _____

   Dictionary: _____

3. mechanical [3]

   Your guess from context: _____

   Dictionary: _____

4. scramble   [12]

   Your guess from context: _____

   Dictionary: _____

5. dumbfounded   [16]

   Your guess from context: _____

   Dictionary: _____

6. deserted [16]

Your guess from context: _____

Dictionary: _____

7. telepathy   [20]

Your guess from context: _____

Dictionary: _____

8. boast [53]

Your guess from context: _____

Dictionary: _____

➤ READING SKILL: Close Reading

In previous units you have developed the reading skills of skimming and scanning and learned how to locate topic and main idea in articles. Reading literature is rather different, however, and requires a reading skill known as "close reading." By close reading we mean slow, careful reading. When we read literature, we don't expect one main idea, but, rather, we find many levels of meaning in the story's plot, setting, and characters.

➤ READING SKILL PRACTICE: Close Reading

Part A: Plot Summary

"Plot" is what happens in the story, its main events. Answer the following questions to review the plot of the story:

1. Who are the main characters?

2. Where are they?

3. What is the situation?

4. The following events are out of order. Put them in order to describe what has happened before this story's time:

   _____ building of the underground city

   _____ Luke often leaves Surreal to go as far as the edge of the tunnel

_____ formation of tribes in Laurania

__1__ the Great Destruction (fire and plague)

5. What things surprise Luke? What things surprise Agatha?

Part B: Setting

"Setting" means where and when the story takes place. The book this story comes from has two settings. Make a list of the differences between Surreal and Laurania. The differences could be in the environment, sounds, food, and so on.

Surreal	Laurania
_____	_____
_____	_____
_____	_____
_____	_____
_____	_____

Part C: Characters

We can understand the main characters by noticing their appearance, behavior, and conversation.

1. What do Luke and Agatha look like?

2. Read the following sentences from the story. Paragraphs are indicated in brackets [ ]. Draw conclusions about Luke's and Agatha's personalities.

Sentences from Story	Your Conclusions about Luke
Luke was off on one of his dangerous adventures.[1]	_____
Lukes's eyes closed, and he waited for death. [4]	_____
"I'm not frightened," Luke answered. [7]	_____
He felt that such a remark might hurt her feelings. [27]	_____
Luke took one politely. [29]	_____

Sentences from Story	Your Conclusions about Agatha
She was shaking with laughter. [12]	_____
The girl's superior tone annoyed him. [17]	_____
The girl flashed a friendly smile. [24]	_____
"From wheat, you idiot! Don't you know anything at all?" [40]	_____

3. Which character, Luke or Agatha, do you prefer, and why? How might their different environments have influenced their characters?

➤ INTERACTIVE JOURNAL RESPONSE

Choose one of the following questions and write a response. Be prepared to give an oral summary of your written response in small groups.

1. What do you think is the author's main reason for writing this story? What does she want to show or teach us?

2. What will happen next to Luke and Agatha? Create a new ending. Be imaginative! Consider these questions:

    Will they return to their societies?

    Will they ever meet again?

    Will they meet regularly and even introduce each other to their families and society?

3. Where do you think you would prefer to live, Surreal or Laurania? Why?

➤ COMMUNICATE: Predicting the Future

Part A: Predict

Predict what the world will be like in 2025. Use the topics from this book to make predictions about the future. Try to think of a positive and a negative prediction for each topic. Then check (✓) the prediction you believe is more likely to happen.

Example

Topic	Positive Prediction	Negative Prediction
Aging	People will live longer, healthier lives and we will have a more stable society.	✓ There won't be enough young people to work and support the aging society.

Topic	Positive Prediction	Negative Prediction
1. Global Village		
2. Tourism		
3. Biodiversity		
4. Love		
5. Time		
6. Green Business		
7. Beauty		
8. Wireless Technology		
9. Media and Culture		
10. Development		
11. Cloning		

Part B: Discuss

Share your predictions with your group.

1. Count how many positive and negative predictions your group has and be ready to tell the class. How positive is your group/your class about the future?

2. Choose the four most interesting predictions to share with the class.

Use the following expressions in your group discussion.

Making predictions	Expressing definite consequences
Maybe there will be . . .	If [x] happens, [y] will happen.
Perhaps the world will . . .	
It's possible the world will . . .	
Probably tourism will . . .	
I predict that there will be . . .	
I'm sure that there will be . . .	
Responding to Ideas	**Expressing possible consequences**
Do you really think so?	If [x] happens, [y] might happen.
That's a good idea!	may
I hope so!	could
I hope not!	
That's a depressing thought.	
What an optimistic view!	

TEXT CREDITS

Page 3, from "The Global Village Finally Arrives," by Pico Iyer. Copyright 1991 by *Time International*. Reprinted by permission. **Page 13**, brochure from Goliath Safaris, Zimbabwe. **Page 21**, "A World of Difference," Anonymous. Reprinted by permission of *Contours*, 1986. **Page 28**, quiz from Teacher's Guide to World Resources, 1992. Reprinted by permission. **Page 28**, from "Trees for Biodiversity, Trees for Life," by Steve Barnes. Reprinted courtesy of the Food and Agriculture Organization of the United Nations, 1991. **Page 35**, from "Diversity in Diet Helps Preserve Species," by Merial Hiramoto, Asahi Evening News. Reprinted by permission. **Page 45**, from "The Basics of Flirting," www.Wesleyan.edu. **Page 67**, from Internet interview "Timeshifting" with author Daniel Redwood. Reprinted by permission. **Page 76**, from "'Rainforest Chic': An Idea Uniting Economy, Ecology" by William R. Long. Copyright 1992 by *Los Angeles Times*. Reprinted by permission. **Page 83**, reprinted courtesy of The Body Shop. **Page 85**, from "Seikatsu: Japanese Housewives Organize" by Shigeki Maruyama, "Green Business: Hope or Hoax?"1991. Reprinted by permission of New Society Publishers. **Page 94**, from "Almond Pedicure: It's a Guy Thing" by Stephen Henderson, *The New York Times*. Copyright 1998 by The New York Times Co. Reprinted by permission. **Page 102**, from "For Many Girls, Gaining Weight is a Rite of Passage," by Ann M. Simmons, Los Angeles Times, copyright 1998. Reprinted by permission. **Page 110**, from "High-Tech Polishes an Old Tradition in Phnom Penh," by Puy Kea, *Kyodo News*. Reprinted by permission. **Page 119**, from "Love those Wearables!," by Stefan Theil, *Newsweek*, April 9, 2001. Copyright 2001, Newsweek, Inc. All rights reserved. Reprinted by permission. **Page 126**, from *Ancient Futures: Learning from Ladakh* by Helena Norberg-Hodge. Copyright 1991. Reprinted by permission. **Page 151**, from *Tomorrow's World*. Reprinted courtesy of Canadian Red Cross Society. **Page 153**, from "Gaviotas: A Village to Reinvent the World," by Alan Weisman, *Mother Jones*. Copyright 1998, Foundation for National Progress. Reprinted by permission. **Page 157**, from "The Most Innovative City in the World,"by Robin Wright, *Los Angeles Times*. Copyright 1996 by *Los Angeles Times*. Reprinted by permission. **Page 166**, from "Dolly's Creators Clone Pigs," by Norm Goldstein, March 14, 2000. Reprinted with permission of The Associated Press. **Page 169**, from "Dolly's False Legacy," by Ian Wilmut. Copyright 1999 by *Time*. Reprinted by permission. **Page 173**, from "Cloning of Man's Best Friend," Nando Media, February 22, 2000. Reprinted with permission of The Associated Press. **Page XXXX**, from "Metaphors for the Future," *Our Present: Their Future* by Barbara Dixon. Copyright ETC Publications. Reprinted by permission. **Page 181**, from *The City Underground* by Suzanne Martel. Copyright 1983 Groundwood Books. Reprinted by permission.

PHOTO CREDITS

Page 1, courtesy of NASA. **Page 11**, Brenda Bushell and Brenda Dyer. **Page 13**, Brenda Bushell and Brenda Dyer. **Page 21**, David & Peter Tumley/Corbis. **Page 27**, Michael & Patricia Fogden/Corbis. **Page 43**, Ronnen Eschel/Corbis. **Page 57**, Francesco Venturi/Corbis. **Page 67**, Corbis. **Page 75**, Karl Weatherly/Corbis. **Page 85**, Brenda Bushell and Brenda Dyer. **Page 93**, Lindsay/Hebbard/Corbis. **Page 94**, Bob Krist/Corbis. **Page 109**, Koichi Kamashida/Getty Images. **Page 110**, Kyodo News International Inc. **Page 119**, Michael Sloan/Newsweek. **Page 125**, John Chiasson/Liaison/Getty Images. **Page 143**, Michael Justice/The Image Works. **Page 153**, Porterfield/Chickering/Photo Researchers. **Page 163**, Stephen Ferry/Liaison/ Getty Images. **Page 179**, ChromoSohm/J. Sohm/The Image Works.

INFORMATION GAPS

Unit 2, Reading One

Partner B

1. You and your partner A want to take a trip. Now you are deciding which country to visit—Canada or Thailand. Both of you have gathered some information on each country, but both of you are missing some information. Find out the missing information by asking your partner questions.

	Canada	Thailand
Language		Thai and some English
Money	Canadian dollar	
Weather	warm in summer, cold in winter	
Food		spicy, with lots of vegetables and fish, served with rice
Places to Visit	Quebec City, Niagara Falls Vancouver and the Rocky Mountains	
What to Wear		shorts, T-shirts, cover your legs and shoulders when visiting temples

Unit 2, Reading Two

Student B

"On my trip this summer to Brazil, I spent my time doing water sports and shopping. I had a great time. Everything was so cheap, and the people in the hotel and the shops were so friendly. They were happy to have my foreign money. Maybe tourists like me change their traditional lifestyle, but I don't think that's any problem. Culture changes. I had a lot of fun and I can't wait to go back next year."